D0786846

GARDEN CITY

GARDEN CITY

Dreams in a Kansas Town

By HOLLY HOPE

UNIVERSITY OF OKLAHOMA PRESS : NORMAN AND LONDON

Library of Congress Cataloging-in-Publication Data

Hope, Holly, 1956–
   Garden City: dreams in a Kansas town / by Holly Hope.
      p.   cm.
   ISBN 0–8061–2105–X (alk. paper)
   1. Garden City (Kan.)—History.   2. Hope, Holly, 1956–
3. Urban-rural migration—Kansas—Garden City.   4. Garden City
(Kan.)—Biography.   5. City and town life—Kansas—Garden City.
I. Title.
F689.G2H675   1988   87-26491
978.1′44—dc19   CIP

The paper in this book meets the guidelines for permanence and durability of the Committee on Production Guidelines for Book Longevity of the Council on Library Resources, Inc.

For my parents

Contents

Illustrations

Maps

Acknowledgments

A PERSON WHO WRITES A BOOK about her hometown has many people to thank. My first thanks, though, must go to three people who have never set foot in Garden City. Rudolph Nelson, Eugene Garber, and Ted Jennings were the first readers of the manuscript. Their enthusiasm and curiosity fell like rain upon parched soil—I thought Kansas the most local, least exotic place in the world. Their support and constructive criticism gave me the courage to explore familiar territory.

A number of people and institutions in Kansas provided valuable information and services. For the agricultural statistics and other factual information that appear in Chapters 1 and 11, I am grateful to Dr. Lawrent Buschman and the late Dr. Mark Hooker, both of the Southwest Kansas Branch Experiment Station; Marcella Degnan, of Agricultural Stabilization and Conservation Services; and the Kansas Water Office. For their help in locating photographs, I thank the Finney County Historical Society and Nancy Sherbert, Curator of Photographs for the Kansas State Historical Society. My editor, John N. Drayton, answered numerous questions and waited patiently during my long pauses of communication.

Several readers helped refine the content of this book. Christopher Currin's criticism of earlier versions of the manuscript made me reevaluate both my own words and my hometown. Where his sensitivity to thought and language overcame my own stubbornness and impatience, the manuscript improved immeasurably. I am grateful also to James F. Hoy for his detailed, perceptive observations and suggestions, and to David Dary for pointing out the quotation from Margaret Stotts, which appears in Chapter 1. The manuscript was meticulously edited by Velma Ivie and Mildred Logan. Any errors that remain are my own.

The second part of this book would not have been possible without those who did go home again—Jay Brown, Doral ("Skip") Mancini, Barbara and Rodney Hoffman, and Dennis Garcia—and who gave generously of their time and life stories. Their courage, perseverance, imagination, and semiarid humor restored my faith in a place I once considered as barren of opportunity as it is of forests. I am grateful also to the staff members of KANZ-FM—Molly Hoffman, Steve Olson, Chuck Lakaytis, Judy Seligson, Shawn Gilson, Linda Trower-Shuss, Rachel Hunter, and Carlene Schweer—for cheerfully taking time out from their sixty-hour work weeks to talk about public radio and western Kansas. And once I could reach him, Quentin Hope, my brother, gave invaluable insights into his own life and projects, as well as the area. Not everyone who has contributed to KANZ or to the community could be included in these pages. My selection is a sample only; no slight is intended to those not mentioned.

Through memory or more direct means, each of my sisters has also contributed to this work. For several months Christine Hope supplied me with a room of my own and a word processor, endured my silence and distraction, and took me to the beach on weekends. Nancy and Rosemary Hope provided me with strong counterpoints through their experiences and reactions to Garden City. Through her birth and childhood, Megan Hope helped me rediscover the things I loved about Garden City when I was her age; she also relayed numerous phone messages for me. My memories, I am sure, do not always match my sisters' in tone, intensity, or detail. I leave them to their own versions.

Special thanks are due my parents, Dolores and Clifford Hope, who for five months housed and fed me while I gathered information and wrote my first draft. Their hospitality and suppertime conversations about their early days in Garden City added an important dimension to my thinking and engendered in me an interest in local history that I had so steadfastly ignored as a child. Later, by long distance, they tracked down addresses, phone numbers, and countless other details for me. Not once did they discourage my efforts, though I trod upon personal ground. If at times during my first eighteen years I doubted the values and intelligence of other Kansans, I always knew that my parents' integrity, sense of humor, love of knowledge, and charity toward others would serve me well in the world beyond Kansas.

HOLLY HOPE

Irving, Texas

PART ONE

In place of the red men and buffalo now extinct now stands Garden City with its hundred thousand people, the Metropolis of South Western Kansas. Tributary to it five million farmers' homes dot the plains. Through a wise policy of tree planting and fruit culture the old northerns gave way to gentle zephyrs. Kindly rains visit us, without disastrous floods, or dreaded drouths. The fame of Western Kansas fruit is wide as the land and broad as the sea. The fruit trains that leave here on its ten railways are the wonder of the world. A soil made richer year after year by irrigation is the first great cause of the change from a seeming desert to lovely gardens the pride of South Western Kansas.

—ONE-HUNDRED-YEAR PREDICTION FROM THE FRONT PAGE OF THE
GARDEN CITY HERALD, MARCH 24, 1883

Crossing the Missouri river into Kansas, the west-bound traveler begins a steady, upward climb, until he reaches the summit of the Rockies. The journey through Kansas covers in four hundred miles nearly five thousand feet of the long, upward slant. In that long hillside there are three or four distinct kinds of landscape, distinguished from one another by the trees that trim the horizon.

The hills and bluffs that roll away from the river are covered with scrub oaks, elms, walnuts, and sycamores. As the wayfarer pushes westward, the oak drops back, then the sycamore follows the walnut, and finally the elm disappears, until three hundred miles to the westward, the horizon of the "gently rolling" prairie is serrated by the scraggy cottonwood, that rises awkwardly by some sandbarred stream, oozing over the moundy land. Another fifty miles, and at Garden City, high up on the background of the panorama, even the cottonwood staggers; and here and there, around some sinkhole in the great flat floor of the prairie, droops a desolate willow—the last weary pilgrim from the lowlands.

—WILLIAM ALLEN WHITE, "A STORY OF THE HIGHLANDS," 1896

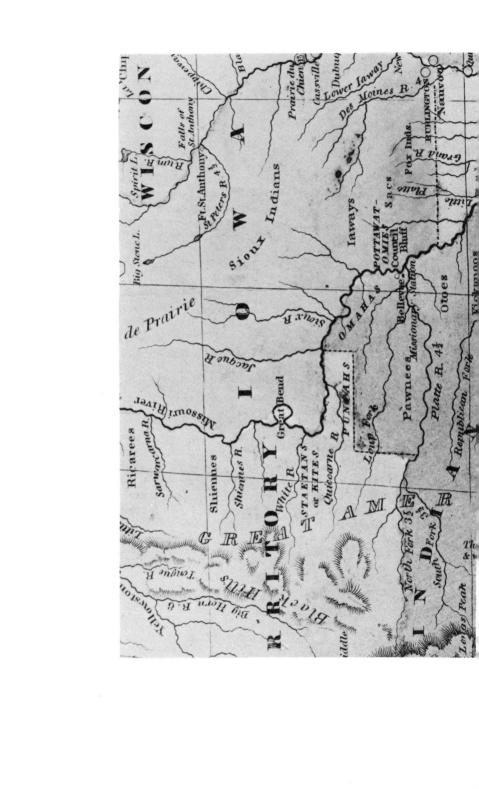

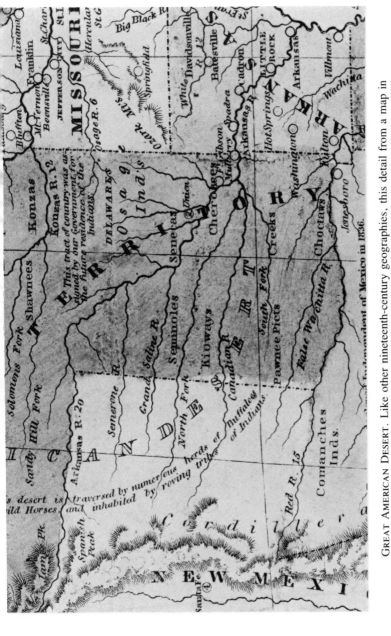

GREAT AMERICAN DESERT. Like other nineteenth-century geographies, this detail from a map in *Olney's School Geography* (1841) attached the label the "Great American Desert" to the unsettled area east of the Rockies. Garden City is located along the Arkansas River, east of the "C" in "AMERICAN." (Courtesy of the Cartographic History Library, Special Collections of the University of Texas at Arlington Libraries, Arlington, Texas)

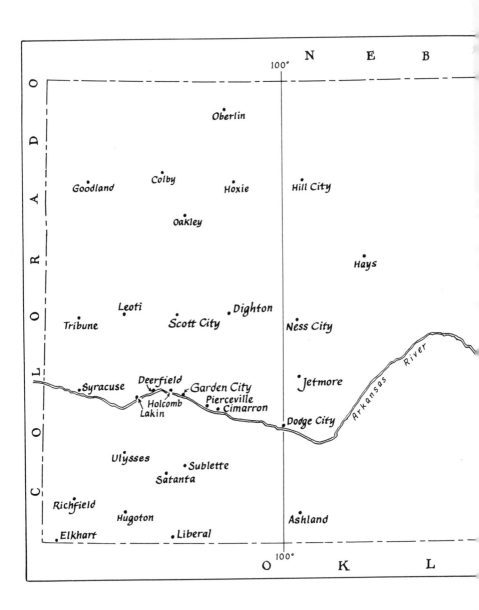

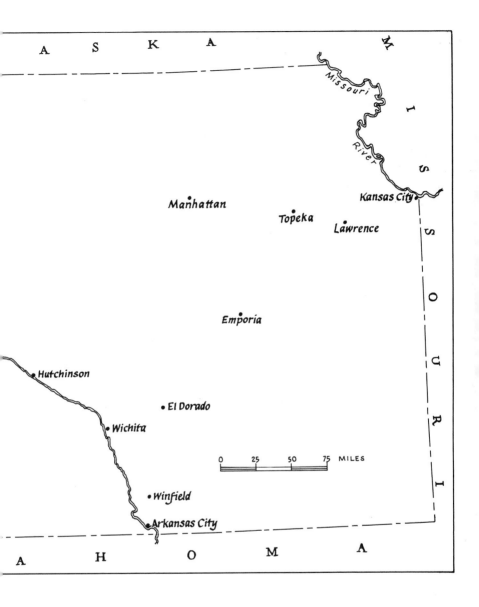

STATE OF KANSAS. If certain members of the 1859 Wyandotte Convention had had their way, the western boundary of Kansas would have passed through Hays. The inclusion of western Kansas within the state boundaries saved Kansans from living in a square state.

CHAPTER I

Pipe Dreams

I GREW UP ON THE HIGH PLAINS, in the rain shadow of the Rocky Mountains, fifty miles west of the hundredth meridian, which according to some accounts is where the West begins. With an average annual rainfall of eighteen inches, the area falls just short of the twenty-inch minimum deemed necessary for growing crops. Subhumid. Semiarid. This land and climate historically have offered the farmer and the entrepreneur a thin margin of hope the other side of prudence and provided me with my first glimpse of the vagaries of nature and the stubbornness of the human spirit blinded by a vision. New York, Michigan, Georgia, Alabama, Texas, Missouri, South Dakota, and Idaho all have towns named Garden City, but Garden City, Kansas—my hometown—was named out of unabashed optimism.

Early visitors to the area stayed long enough only to mutter a few discouraging words. In 1541, Coronado and his men crossed the High Plains in search of Quivira, the legendary city of gold. Instead they found nomadic Indians and villages of straw huts in what is thought to be present-day Kansas. An Indian had led them there, hoping they would starve to death on the way. No gold, no slaves, it was a land where they could see sky between the legs of a buffalo and march several thousand strong without denting the grass. Coming from a semiarid land himself, Coronado noted the agricultural possibilities of the area; but he had not traveled across an ocean for farmland. Kansas was not Peru. The Spanish were not interested.

Almost three centuries later the reports were not as generous. On his 1806 expedition to the Rocky Mountains, Zebulon Pike compared the Plains to the deserts of Africa. Stephen Long's unpublished map of 1823 labeled this region the "Great Desert." During the 1840s and 1850s popular atlases and geographies prominently displayed the "Great American Desert" over the area that is now northern Texas, western Oklahoma, western Kansas, and eastern Colorado.

That appellation set western Kansas apart, marking it as an area geographically and culturally distinct from the rest of the state to which it would belong. At the 1859 Wyandotte Convention, delegates from what would soon become eastern Kansas were among the most vehement detractors of the land west of them. One participant suggested that the western boundary of the state extend no farther than Hays (140 miles east of the Kansas-Colorado border and northeast of present-day Garden City). Others argued that the state should be square—homogeneous in climate, soil, and occupation.

The railroads beat the settlers to western Kansas. In the 1840s the frontier had leaped almost two thousand miles across the Plains to the well-watered and wooded Oregon territory. For the settlers and the gold seekers after them, the Plains were only a highway to the Pacific Coast or the Rocky Mountains, a proving ground of courage and endurance, a dumping ground for possessions too heavy and bones too weary. The best-known immigration route, the Oregon Trail, bypassed what is now western Kansas altogether; only the Santa Fe Trail, a commercial trade route, followed the Arkansas River through this forbidding territory.

When the construction of a transcontinental railroad began, however, the middle started filling in. Between 1862 and 1882 more homestead claims were filed (and more reneged) in Kansas than in any other state in the country. Eastern Kansas claimed the first settlers; western Kansas got the latecomers— the immigrants, the gamblers, the desperate. Only the powerful rhetoric of the railroad pamphlets and the promise of cheap land could lure folks to make this land swept of trees their destination. With the stroke of a pen the Great American Desert became the Garden.

Civilization was on its way. In 1873 the Kansas legislature named Sequoyah County (for the Cherokee Indian); settlers, however, did not start arriving until the moist spring of 1878. In 1879, Sequoyah County, along with other territory, was organized into a municipal township, but it remained under the jurisdiction of Ford County for the next five years. In 1884 the area was organized as a county and renamed "Finney," much to the relief of most residents, who favored the easier spelling and pronunciation, according to Leola Howard Blanchard's book, *Conquest of Southwest Kansas*. That same year Garden City was declared the county seat.

Blanchard depicts life in early-day Garden City as harsh and mean. To survive, many settlers picked up buffalo and cattle bones and shipped them by rail for five or six dollars a ton. They used buffalo chips for fuel in winter, caught wild horses and shipped them east, and hunted antelope. Margaret Emma Stotts describes her experience as an early-day settler in the "garden":

> . . . The spring and summer we came here, 1881, was very dry. For nine consecutive months there was not a single drop of rain. There were no trees. Some cottonwood cuttings had been set out along the streets of Garden City, but as yet furnished no shade, and the soap weeds, the largest thing here, furnished very little.
>
> Each day the sun arose in a blaze of glory, each succeeding day more dazzling than the one before. We kept our eyes turned heavenward looking for clouds, not being so presumptuous as to expect rain, but merely seeking a dimmer for the intense sunlight. We saw in the mirage limpid lakes of sparkling water, buildings which might have been churches and theaters, and beautiful groves of stately trees, but it all kept just out of reach and the blazing sun shone on. The certainty that it would be on the job again in the morning took away the pleasure of its setting.

The drought mentioned by Stotts continued into 1882. During the brief respite of the following five years, the population of Finney County grew, reaching over eight thousand by 1887.

But another drought followed, and the population had dropped to under three thousand by 1891.

Over the years various ways of dealing with the water shortage on the Plains were tried. In 1906 the federal government established a National Forest Reserve, consisting of 165,000 acres, in Finney County and four neighboring counties. One million trees were planted the first year, and similar numbers were planted the next several years. This doomed effort grew out of a belief that rain followed trees; that is, if the area looked more like land that received a lot of rain, it would rain. Others believed that rain followed the plow and set to planting every available acre. Some farmers actually learned a few things about the land and the climate. Plowing the soil after every rain conserved moisture. Wheat, particularly Turkey Red brought by the Mennonites, and alfalfa grew better than corn. Those bent on more immediate profit tried more spectacular solutions: balloons, box kites, and dynamite were all used to coax rain from the sky. Like the Indian who led the Spaniards to Quivira, the rainmakers would lead the farmers to cloudy skies and prosperity.

In southwest Kansas, though, it was the businessman, rather than the inventor, who, by concentrating on the consumption of available water rather than the production of new water, would win the patronage of farmers and a name for Garden City as an irrigation center. As early as 1879 the first canal was built along the Arkansas River. Other canals followed, extending for ten, twenty, and even forty miles and bearing such names as the Amazon and the Great Eastern. They were not very successful: the crude canals clogged with weeds, much of the water evaporated, and the flow of the river was inconsistent—from flash floods to a modest stream. To make matters worse, by 1902 farmers upstream in eastern Colorado had started irrigating their crops with water from the Arkansas, lessening the flow even more.

When the river was low, some farmers became miners of water, going underground to the alluvium directly beneath the riverbed and the aquifer that underlies much of the area. The supply seemed endless. "All you have to do is pull up a beet, stick a pump in the hole and go to pumping," A. W. Stubbs told C. J. ("Buffalo") Jones, a founder of Garden City, according to the first volume of *Finney County History*. That seemed to be the attitude characteristic of most settlers: If the sky and their neighbors upstream were stingy, then surely the ground would be good to them. In 1905 the U.S. Reclamation Service approved a major project to pump the water underneath the riverbed out into the ditches. By 1908 a central power station and twenty-three pump stations, placed at thousand-feet intervals, were in operation. (Two years later, however, when it was estimated that most of the water was lost through evaporation and seepage from the ditches, the project was closed.) Elsewhere in the area windmills flecked the landscape, pumping water from as much as ninety feet below and putting the tireless wind to use.

But irrigation had its limits and nature its revenge. For six consecutive years, from 1934 to 1939, the rainfall in Garden City averaged more than seven and a half inches below normal. Added to the wind and the indiscriminate plowing of the earth, the drought caused more dust and people to blow across the country than ever before. Even so, some folks stuck to the area, like tumbleweeds caught in a barbed-wire fence. With the help of the federal government and an obliviousness to grit, they pulled through to 1940, when the rainfall total was 1.28 inches above average.

By the 1950s the population of Garden City was over ten thousand and growing. Through irrigation western Kansas had established itself as respectable farm country, and Kansas was calling itself the breadbasket of the world. For a time in the mid-1950s a drought threatened to return the western part of the state to the dust-bowl days. In 1954 a dust storm worse than any of those during the 1930s blew through Garden City at seventy miles an hour; and 1956, the year I was born, is the driest year on record at the Garden City Agricultural Experiment Station: 5.68 inches. But the drought was short-lived. Kansas's native son Ike, recently reelected president, visited and promised relief, and the following year nature provided its own: twenty-one inches of rain. For me dust storms were no more than yellowed black-and-white photographs and my mother's love of rainy days. The locust plagues of the latter part of the nineteenth century were funny postcards of giant grasshoppers; the cattle kingdom was the odor of manure from a nearby feedyard. I grew up thinking that I lived in the heart of the self-sufficient, complacent Midwest, praying in church every Sunday for rain, and believing in the name of my hometown.

There was some horticultural evidence to warrant that belief. By the time I was born, shade trees blocked out the relentless sun from most of the town. Gillespie Place, where my family and I lived on the east end of town, was particularly cool and shady. American and Chinese elm, locust, and walnut trees lined either side of the street, their branches arching high overhead and sometimes touching. That each tree on our block and in the rest of Garden City had been specifically, deliberately planted did not strike me as odd. Trees were precious: it was their presence, not their absence, that warranted explanation.

Across town lawns required and received similar care. Yards in the older, shadier parts of town were covered with cool bluegrass, while soft bermuda grass grew around the newer houses. Residents used the latest in lawn-care equipment—power lawn mowers and sprinkler systems. That such care, time, and technology are not expended everywhere across the country on lawns in middle-class neighborhoods has always jarred me a little as an adult. In upstate New York I laughed the first time I saw a neighbor using a small electric mower with a cord trailing behind it. Visiting my sister in South Carolina, I marveled that lawns of grass, vines, and flowers grew with no manual or mechanical watering. And when I lived in central Illinois I was dismayed upon seeing the brown, wilted, unwatered lawns of mid-August. Clearly the residents did not fear being told that they lived in a desert.

Perhaps more than any place else I knew, my grandfather's yard manifested the vision of the garden. He grew only one crop—roses—but in great abundance (around three hundred bushes) and in great variety, marking each kind with little metal signs: Camelot, Peace, Tiffany, Mr. Lincoln, American Beauty, Ma Perkins, and a special lavender rose of which he was so proud. The dry heat of the Kansas summer was hard on them, but he took special precautions: mulching the soil with clean grass clippings and adding layers of cottonseed hulls in midsummer, soaking the bushes with cloth hoses to keep the roots moist, and cutting the blooms only in the cool of the evening or in the early morning.

In between bushes he laid down a stone pathway so that each plant could be attended to easily. Before adding fertilizer he analyzed the soil to determine all the deficiencies, and to protect the roses from the harsh wind, he had a fence built in the backyard. When it proved to be too solid, trapping the heat of the summer in the northwest corner of the yard, he had it rebuilt, leaving spaces between the boards for air circulation. He sprayed for bugs and blights, stooping or even lying on the ground to get underneath the leaves. Sometimes my siblings and I helped out by collecting ladybugs to eat the aphids. Winters were not always severe, but, just in case, he put mounds of sand and soil around the bases of the bushes to insulate the roots. When people praised his roses, I was nonchalant. But secretly I loved them: the velvet-soft petals that pressed against my nose when I sniffed too hard, the tightly furled blooms that I could squeeze without hurting, and the innermost glow of yellow that could not be seen until the rose had spread itself wide.

Elsewhere around town more public evidence of the garden could be found. South of town, near the houses of the Mexican Americans, for instance, was Finnup Park. Donated in 1919 by the son of an early settler, the park served primarily as a picnic and campground. Then in 1922 a swimming pool was opened—not just any pool, but what, with many qualifying adjectives, was claimed to be the world's largest swimming pool. Half a city block long and holding close to three million gallons of water, it required two days to drain and fill. When my father was growing up, no fence surrounded the pool; you could swim any time of the day or night—as long as you were not Mexican. A bathhouse, wading pool, fence, lifeguards, and hours had been added by the time I swam there, and anyone could swim—free. Sufficiently waterlogged, you could walk over to Kansas's largest zoo, opened in 1927. The nearest, perhaps the only, rival was the Wichita zoo, some two hundred miles away. Kids in surrounding towns grew up with cats and dogs and, if they lived in the country, maybe chickens and horses. But in Garden City my friends and I grew up knowing Penny, the elephant; Tela, the hippo; Stan and Lyn, the polar bears; stately lions and tigers; stonelike alligators; beady-eyed ostriches and emus; delicately boned white-tailed deer and antelope; and peacocks that strutted freely all over the zoo. I felt lucky to live in a town that could boast so many superlatives.

How odd, it seems to me now, that in this vision of the town, where people took pains to grow trees and roses, to construct an enormous watering hole, and to import exotic animals, the Arkansas River had no place. As a source for irrigation, of course, its significance had been realized. But as a resource for recreational and aesthetic pleasure, it literally did not hold much water. As a child I joined in the jokes made about the lazy trickle beneath the long bridge on Highway 83, south of Garden City. Sometimes on the Fourth of July there was enough water in which to wade, skip stones, and shoot off firecrackers in pop cans. And once in June, 1965, after heavy rains to the west, it leaped its banks and soaked the zoo and the south end of town. But much of the time we had to look hard among the weeds to see the dwindling stream.

Yet when the river disappeared altogether, I was caught off guard. Visiting in 1979, I took a drive along the river road, west of town. The cottonwoods stood like skeletons, their trunks as smooth and white as bones, their branches leafless claws. Weeds choked the riverbed. I could not recall the last time I had seen water in the riverbed. Checking around, I found there had been none since 1975.

Even the name itself seemed to be gone. Natives of Kansas have always pronounced it "ar·kan′ sas." But around town in the early 1980s, I heard people saying "ar′ kan·saw"—like the state. Some of the newcomers, I daresay, did not even know there ever was a river.

While the disappearance of the river coincided with the loss of its name, the imminent disappearance of another source of water has brought an unfamiliar name into popular use: the Ogallala Aquifer. Extending over 180,000 square miles underneath parts of South Dakota, Nebraska, Kansas, Colorado, Oklahoma, Texas, and New Mexico, the Ogallala holds one-third as much water as Lake Superior. Not as accessible as water in a lake, the water from the aquifer must be pumped from saturated thicknesses of clay, silt, sand, and gravel. Throughout the century folks in western Kansas have boasted of this seemingly inexhaustible source of underground water without bothering to learn its name. When it began to appear that their hopes were based on a mirage, however, the name started appearing in newspapers and conversations, even on T-shirts.

The consumption of water accelerated greatly in the late 1960s, when several farmers in western Kansas began using a technology that made pumping water from the aquifer easier and more profitable. Known as center-pivot irrigation, it operates by means of a deep-well turbine pump, which is situated in the center of a field. The water spurts out two long, raised sprinkler arms that are rolled across the field in a circle. Within ten years of the introduction of the center-pivot, the number of acres under irrigation in western Kansas tripled. Irrigation became a three-billion-dollar-a-year business, and corn became a major crop—a pipe dream that surpassed the visions of even the most wildly optimistic promoter of the late 1800s.

The irrigators' success in growing corn attracted other water-intensive industries. In the late 1970s and early 1980s, Iowa Beef Processors located what is claimed to be the world's largest meat-packing plant just west of Garden City. It is an efficient arrangement: cattle are fattened in area feedlots on feed grain—particularly corn—grown in nearby fields; then they are brought to Iowa Beef, where they are killed, butchered, and packaged. IBP has brought new jobs, new people, and prosperity to the area. But it also requires a lot of water. Early projections claimed that IBP would use no more water than would irrigating the equivalent acreage owned by the plant, though the demand would be steadier than that of irrigation, extending across the entire year rather than just the growing season. And, of course, IBP's dependence on irrigated crops further increases the area's dependence on irrigation.

While yielding a greater profit, corn also requires twenty-four inches of water a year—more than sorghum or soybeans or wheat, and six inches more than the annual rainfall average—and a pumping rate of nine hundred to twelve hundred gallons a minute. During these years the withdrawal rate grew to fourteen times the recharge rate, and the water table dropped by several feet a year. Because the aquifer is deeper in some places than in others, the consequences of this depletion have been felt differently. Some wells have already gone dry, while others still have plenty. But none is limitless. The slogan of the Populists in the 1890s called on Kansans to raise less corn and more hell. In light of the fate of the aquifer and the river, the slogan of the 1980s should demand that irrigators in western Kansas stop raising corn, or other western Kansans will start raising hell.

Prophets foresaw—and warned against—this situation decades before. In 1901 geologist Willard Johnson prepared the definitive description of the geology of the High Plains for the U.S. Geological Survey. Thirty years later historian Walter Prescott Webb drew upon this report in his book *The Great Plains:* "The suggestion of reclamation by irrigation from ground water is based upon the assumption that the rate of supply is sufficient for the demands of extensive irrigation; but such utilization over a broad area would call for a re-supply 'beyond the possibilities of the most humid climate.' " In 1958 another government report on the Cimarron Basin voiced concerns about depletion.

Having their choice of government studies, many irrigators seem to have taken the more sanguine view of the State Geological Survey of Kansas in August, 1944: "This regional lowering of the water table probably will be very slight for the amount of water in underground storage is very large." In the copy of this report at the Garden City Public Library, someone has underlined this statement and scrawled underneath it, "Greed is not taken into account, however."

But greed is not restricted to farmers in western Kansas. In the summer of 1982, as I was traveling west from Garden City on the train, I was reminded of the advantages of living upstream. Around Lakin, Kansas, twenty miles east of Garden City, water began to appear in the Arkansas riverbed. Volunteer alfalfa and sunflowers grew wild, the cottonwoods were alive, and woolly-headed bushes, like huge broccoli flowerets, were perched on the banks. Beyond the Colorado line, where the farmland is even more marginal, water from the Arkansas filled a large reservoir. According to a 1948 interstate compact, Kansas is entitled to 40 percent of this water in the John Martin Reservoir. But in recent years another reservoir in south-central Colorado, near Trinidad, has been built on one of the tributaries of the Arkansas. Since 1980 farmers in western Kansas have complained that officials in Colorado have illegally withheld water from them. In Colorado, a western state, water rights are well established, while in Kansas, usually considered a midwestern state, land rights have always been considered more important. Without water-law specialists, western Kansas farmers are going upstream without a paddle.

The problem of water is a question not so much of quantity as of distribution. Water does cover 70 percent of the earth's surface, after all, and it does fall from the sky—a fact more apparent east of Garden City, in central Kansas, where the Arkansas reappears. There the groundwater management district has adopted a policy of not pumping more water from the ground than can be replenished, while the groundwater management district in western Kansas has determined that a 40 percent depletion of the groundwater supply by the end of the century is the acceptable rate of pumping. The difference is not one of virtue but one of rainfall. It rains more in central

Kansas, so farmers there do not need to irrigate as much, and the water table is replenished faster. With less rain, farmers in western Kansas depend on irrigation more, and the water table is replenished more slowly. Even in the years of above-average rainfall, other factors work against recharge in western Kansas: the temperatures are usually hotter, so more rain evaporates; in many places the aquifer is deeper in the ground, so it takes longer for the recharge process to work; and the recharge is slower through the loamy soils of western Kansas than through the sandier soils of central Kansas.

Irrigation grew out of a simple need: water for crops. For people in western Kansas, it has been the one way to compensate for not living near the source of the river or having enough rain. Irrigation, the means of prosperity in this area for several decades, may now be the means of its collapse.

According to a 1982 federal study on the aquifer, change is imminent on the High Plains. Over the next forty years gradual reversion to dryland farming and less thirsty and lucrative crops is expected in Kansas. Because of water-supply problems and prohibitive pumping costs, by 2020 the number of acres devoted to irrigated crops will have declined by 41 percent to 90 percent over 1977 levels (depending on which of four scenarios is followed). The economic effects on the area will depend on market prices and how quickly the transition is made. The aquifer will continue to be depleted, though the rate of decline is expected to be less than in the years prior to 1977. The study does offer one rain-follows-the-plow sort of solution for aiding the aquifer: a multibillion-dollar series of canals and pipelines to transport massive quantities of "surplus" water hundreds of miles from the Missouri, White, Arkansas, Red, Sulphur, Sabine, and Ouachita rivers to the High Plains (no surplus is known to exist).

Garden and desert—the extremes have made Garden City subject to geographical schizophrenia. Its eighteen-inch average rainfall places it in the West, but the variation from year to year—eleven inches in 1954, twenty-one inches in 1955, six inches in 1956, twenty-one inches in 1957, twenty-eight inches in 1958—plays tricks on even the most prudent souls.

The wet years, the dry years—which are the norm, which the mirage?

Wishful thinkers have always aligned Kansas with the Midwest. The settlers brought with them the laws, the agriculture, and the aesthetic of a land with water. Cultivation and civilization, for the most part, were imported and imposed upon the land rather than developed from its elements. According to the theory, the accoutrements of a humid climate—trees and corn and flowers—would force the land itself to adapt, to become more "seasonable."

As a child I accepted that aesthetic readily. I grew up loving what was scarce in western Kansas: rain and trees and roses. I turned off westerns on TV: a hot, dusty world of mostly men, it seemed to me. Boot Hill, in Dodge City, fifty miles east, was a re-creation of a time well gotten over with. Garden City was more civilized than Dodge City, I thought. Days when I could no longer deny where I lived, when the hot, dry wind blew grit in my eyes and tangled my hair, when the parched earth cracked into pieces of a jigsaw puzzle, and when the odor of manure hung in the air, I stayed inside and dreamed about living somewhere else.

On my visits home in recent years, however, I have sensed a change in Garden City's primary aesthetic. The town seems decidedly more western than when I was growing up—even in terms of vegetation. Several years ago I noticed some residents had dug out corners of their front lawns and planted yucca. Yucca. Such an unfriendly plant, with its stiff, pointed leaves that can prick the skin and draw blood—I was offended. Obviously these people had not winced in geography class when western Kansas was labeled semiarid. Still, given the prognosis of the Ogallala, I could see the logic: in an effort to look like Iowa, the area may end up looking like Nevada, so yuccas are in order. They were merely giving in to the inevitable.

I have since learned that the yucca in western Kansas is not that of the desert but is special to the Plains. Also called soapweed or Spanish bayonet, it is a hardy plant—and useful: in earlier days it was used to make soap, rope, and flour. In

bloom along the highway, the white, bulb-shaped flowers—
the plant's one concession to more conventional beauty—appear as naturally as sunflowers. I would like to think they are
a sign that people there are finally adapting to the land and the
climate, becoming more seasonable.

Having lived in places drenched with rain and crowded with
trees and people, I have come to appreciate what I once took
for granted: uncluttered horizons, clarity of sky, muted colors
of buffalo grass and winter wheat, stillness, lack of distraction. The beauty of the High Plains is not obvious: it lacks the
grandeur and sculpture of mountains, the color and flamboyance of the tropics. It evokes in me not the gasp of surprise or
delight but rather the sigh of familiarity and longing. For me
the beauty it offers is personal and inexplicable, as immune to
translation as love for my family. When strangers mock Kansas, call it flat and monotonous and colorless, I sometimes
bristle, but I am not much interested in changing their minds.

I still love rain, and I still hate wind and dust. And I do not
live in Garden City anymore. But I keep in touch, interested
not only in the fate of the aquifer but also in the annual rainfall
totals and individual showers. If nothing else, western Kansas
is a good place in which to develop a thirst.

CHAPTER 2

Books and Pools

MY IDEA OF THE GOOD LIFE has long been a book-filled house facing the ocean, a sort of library along the shore. This dream began during my childhood summers in Kansas, where you could read or swim all day without feeling that you were missing much. Once school was out, days became as indistinguishable as wheat rows stretching out to the horizon, and I immersed myself in my favorite elements: words and water.

Reading was an unqualified good in my home—a quiet pleasure, not requiring special equipment or adult supervision. The glass doors of the built-in china cabinet in the dining room were removed to make room for more books; magazines and newspapers accumulated on coffee tables and chairs until my mother took a stack to a neighbor or to a doctor's office. Even the rest of the household hesitated to interrupt a member of the family who was embarked on a story.

Though there was plenty to read in my house, I usually chose to get my books elsewhere. Most often I went to the town library. My oldest sister, Chris, worked there, so I knew the librarians: the red-haired woman who worked in the basement repairing books; the younger one of slight build and the grandmotherly one with a cracked voice who checked out books; and the head librarian with blond curls and a storytelling voice. The procedure for checking out a book was simple: you signed your name to a card tucked in the pocket of the book. When I was very young, though, the name—Garden City *Public* Library—perplexed me. Where did the Democrats get their books?

When I first began going to the library, it was situated on Cedar Street, between Main and Seventh. The ten-block walk there seemed just far enough, with low walls of rock and concrete to balance on, a big black dog and wasps' nests to avoid, and cats to coax across a yard. Two older sisters and a brother accompanied me on those first few walks. Later, when the library moved south a few blocks, friends served as companions. Bumpity, bumpity, our bikes would rattle as we rode down Seventh Street, one of the few streets paved with bricks.

Once I was in the library my companions did not matter. I headed for the walls of books, and my treasure hunt began. Sometimes I followed the grade recommendations taped on the shelves; sometimes I chose a book suggested by a sister (especially if it had made her cry); but more often I conducted my own examination of covers, illustrations, descriptions glued inside covers, sample passages, and even smells to determine which I would carry home. My favorites were about animals and other nonhumans or children who had unusual adventures—a little girl sliding down her bathtub drain into a jungle and the like. Westerns were the only books that I recall rejecting automatically. They brought to mind wind and dust, of which I had plenty already. I preferred to read about places with water and trees and things green, especially on days when the temperature crept over a hundred degrees and the grass turned brown and brittle.

During the school year I raided the shelves in the back of the classroom. Each class had its own small library, so selection was limited but all the more precious. Because I might never see the book again after that year, I read it over and over to make sure I never forgot it, much like the characters in *Fahrenheit 451*. One year my favorite book was about a girl who lived in a house with two gardens—a neatly manicured display in front, a wild, unkempt jungle in back. She preferred the latter, which contained a lion who swallowed her ill-tempered cousin one day. Later, in Europe, when I learned of

the difference between French and English gardens, I thought
of the two gardens in that book.

The textbooks used in school were less pleasing. At the beginning of the year they had to be covered, usually with rough,
dull-brown paper bags from the grocery store. Despite the covers, they still looked worn out by the time I received them: the
corners were frayed or taped, the edges of the pages worn
smooth. Geography books were the largest, filled with facts
for which I had no context. Science books made natural phe-
nomena uninteresting and mechanical operations perplexing.
Even readers were dull, asking questions I didn't care about.
Reading textbooks was a chore. Glad as I was at the end of the
school year to turn them in, I was also anxious, fearing that
the book-rental women would charge my parents for the stray
pen marks and torn pages there from previous years.

An even less aesthetic encounter occurred in fifth grade,
when my school started a packaged reading series. In a corner
of the room sat a large box filled with hierarchically arranged,
color-coded stories printed on white cardboard. Before you
could advance to the next color, you had to read all the stories
for the previous color and answer questions for each on a score
sheet. The teacher placed me in green, below the colors of
many of my friends, so I was behind from the beginning. I
dreaded those periods—people bobbing up and down as they
finished their stories and started others while I was still struggling through my first, the threat of the passing minutes ticking
in my head, the pages that would not bend, and the anxiety
over which questions would be asked when I finished. That
was not reading to me.

Aside from that experience, though, reading was a habitual,
enjoyable aspect of my existence. It allowed me to take in the
outside world at my own rate. I could be in two worlds at
once—petting a cat in my backyard with one hand and holding
a book about children who said "hullo" in another. Later when
I remembered or reread a passage from the book, I might feel
the softness of the cat's fur between my fingers once again or
see the shadow of tree leaves dance on the page, so close was
the connection between imagined and real worlds.

The best time for reading was summer, when I could choose my own books and read at leisure. The library offered book clubs for each grade. The summer after first grade I was a Squeegy Bug, the next year a Book Worm, and in later years a member of the Mary Poppins and Peanuts reading clubs. Each club had its own set of charts and stickers to keep a record of all the books members read that summer. Some kids were competitive, their charts so dotted with stickers that they had to start a second chart and later a third. Sometimes I envied them. Rumor had it, though, that some of the speed readers read very easy books or had their mothers write their reports for them. The first summer was my most prolific— seventy-seven books—the total diminishing in succeeding years as I became absorbed in more difficult books.

The stickers and charts were fun, but mostly I think it was the simplicity of reading that appealed to me. Other skills— tying a shoe, riding a bike, roller skating—I was slow and awkward at learning, but reading required only vision and imagination. No knots to unravel, no sidewalk bumps to avoid, no scrapes to disinfect—reading promised hours of accident-free adventures. I can see myself now: book in hand, head in book, sitting on the gently rocking front-porch swing with my knees up, oblivious to calls for supper. I was for the moment suspended.

Swimming required more paraphernalia than reading, but for the most part I liked it. No hand-me-downs, for one thing. Each summer my mother bought me a new swimsuit and thongs, and every few summers a new beach towel. By August the suit had lost its elasticity and had become snagged or faded, depending on the material; but at the beginning of the summer it was bright and crisp, promising a slightly different tanning pattern from the previous year's swimsuit. (My neighbor and I thought bikinis were risqué—even those Sears sold for toddlers; two-piece suits were all right, we thought, as long as the navel was covered.) Balls, rafts, innertubes, and other equipment were optional. Nose plugs and swimming caps I scorned. The whole idea of swimming, after all, was to be as unencumbered by clothing and baggage as possible.

Primordially, swimming was a whole-body thirst for water. Days when our mothers were too busy to take us to the pool, my neighbor and I ran through sprinklers, jumping over the ropes of water spewed by my family's walking sprinkler or dancing through the spherical spray of her family's ground sprinklers. At other times when my mother used the old pump across our driveway to flood the yard, we waded through the water, catching grass between our toes. If all else failed, we sprayed one another with a hose. But all were poor substitutes for total immersion.

For that we had to go out of the neighborhood. Early-day citizens had provided Garden City with a swimming pool, unrivaled in size or accessibility. Started as a public works project in the early 1920s, the pool turned into a whole-town affair. Workers, merchants, and horse teams kept digging until the pool was 220 feet wide and 330 feet long—thirty feet longer than a football field. In those days people referred to it modestly as the "Old Swimming Hole"; the postcards and signs during my childhood proclaimed it the "world's largest, free, concrete, municipal swimming pool." Locals of my day called it simply the "Big Pool."

It was too big, I thought as a child—especially on swimming-lesson days when, standing on the side of the pool at nine in the morning, most of my flesh exposed, I looked out at the forbidding vastness of dark, unrippled water. And often it was too cold. The Big Pool had no filter and so was closed every other Sunday and Monday while it was drained and filled. The Tuesday after it was filled, the water, as yet unwarmed by the afternoon sun, was so cold that just looking at it made the hair on my arms and legs stand up. Alternate Tuesday mornings I lay in bed, praying for rain and hoping the man on the radio would say that swimming lessons had been canceled.

Had that been my only exposure to swimming, I think I would have been as traumatized as my oldest sister. Because our Great-Aunt Mildred worked for the local chapter of the Red Cross, the children in my family were obliged to take the free swimming lessons they offered at the Big Pool. For Chris, who did not know how to swim before she started taking lessons, it meant a cruel plunge into an alien element; for me, it was more a matter of poor timing. I already knew how to swim, from Chris, who, despite her own aversion to the water, had taught me how during hot afternoons when I wanted to be in the water. Swimming lessons were just an ordeal to go through to please adults, like having to eat a big breakfast before you developed an appetite for the day. After they were over, I warmed my blue, shivering body in the bathtub. By afternoon I was ready to plunge into the pool in earnest.

Oddly, that plunge was back into bath water. Heated pools were in vogue in the 1960s. My parents, perhaps softened by their older children's hardships with the Big Pool and on a little steadier financial ground, relented with us younger children and bought a summer membership in the Wheatlands Motel swimming pool. Small and warm, it provided a more intimate atmosphere that gave me the courage to paddle to the deep end or climb up the ramp to the sun deck and jump off.

We had swum there only a summer or two when the Elks built a pool close to our home. Bigger than the Wheatlands pool or the Country Club pool, the Elks offered challenges more easily mastered than those of the Big Pool. For a few summers I stayed close to the four-foot mark, occasionally venturing up the blue-and-white plastic rope that marked off the deep end. One summer, however, my parents let me take swimming lessons there. When I saw the pool without the rope, I began to move more assuredly between the deep end and the shallow end, sometimes diving off the board and swimming the length of the pool underwater.

True independence, though, came at age ten, when my friends and I were allowed into the pool unaccompanied by an adult. No longer did we have to beg our mothers to finish their chores and take us swimming. We could take off on foot or bike any afternoon we pleased. There was hardly an evening when my swimsuit was not hanging on the clothesline. Usually we tried to take along a little change to buy long planks of pink-and-white taffy that softened in the sun or a soft drink with crushed ice. On rare occasions, after a long afternoon of swimming, my mother would let me stay and eat a charbroiled hamburger for supper. Those days both hunger and thirst were satisfied.

My appetite for reading also increased when I started buying my own books. There were no bookstores in town while I was in grade school, but book clubs offered paperbacks through the school. For twenty-five, thirty, or forty cents I could buy a book all my own, write my name in it, and not have to share it with my brother and sisters. The day the order blanks came I would pore over the book descriptions, comparing my choices with the birthday money and allowances I had saved. When the books arrived several weeks later, I could barely remember what I had ordered, and so the occasion was like Christmas. Stroking the smooth covers of each book, riffling the pages and causing what looked like sawdust to spill on my desk, sniffing the fresh glue, I welcomed the chance to break in my own books. Cracked spines, bent corners, and worn covers—those were the signs of a well-read book.

Late in elementary school I developed a passion for mysteries. I read single mysteries and series—Nancy Drew, Cherry Ames, and the Dana Girls. They fed an appetite for things hidden and secret, for pasts unknown and treasures lost. Appearances were belied, things not always what they seemed. Though full of coincidences and neat solutions, they did allow me to plunge for a few hours into darker realms.

Even more, though, I think the series binge was the result of a preadolescent burst of energy. Quantity was the main objective. The plots were predictable (after reading several), the range of emotions called upon was limited, and even the number of pages had been determined in advance. The heart and eye could skim over two in an afternoon. My reading habits changed accordingly: I never read a series book twice, I never owned one, and I had no favorites.

In seventh grade I conformed my taste to what the popular girls read: teenage romances. I bought and read paperbacks about senior proms, unrequited love, and teenage pregnancies. A sideline was books about hairdos and hygiene, from which I learned about using various kitchen ingredients—eggs, vinegar, and mayonnaise—on my hair and how many girdles I should own.

The only book I recall reading over and over during my junior-high years was a less contemporary teenage romance—*Romeo and Juliet.* Zefferelli's film version opened when I was in seventh grade, and I saw it through tears three times. I bought and read the play, hung up posters from the film in my room, learned the theme music on the piano (to accompany a friend who was reciting the prologue for a contest), played the record from the film, and even bought a Juliet-style dress. When we read the play in an English class, my classmates and I corrected the teacher's pronunciation of the names. Never was a story of such woe more read, listened to, memorized, and lamented.

Two years later, another popular book and movie romance, *Love Story,* evoked a much different response. I read it out of curiosity—to see what all the girls in my study hall were sobbing about. When I went with a group of girls to see the film, I found myself laughing at the girls who started crying with the first line. Tired of hiding my books from amused parents and older siblings and surfeited with sentiment, I suppose, I had lost my taste for adolescent romances. Reading about them had done nothing to aid my quest for popularity—my original aim. I read more quickly and more than those who were popular. A short time later I donated all of my paperback romances, with the exception of *Romeo and Juliet,* to a garage sale, wishing I had spent those years reading the unabridged version of *David Copperfield* and the like, as my oldest sister had.

During those same years my interest in swimming waned. Jobs cut into free time, some of my new friends did not know how to swim, and those who did go to the pool had a different purpose: sunbathing. I liked the effects of the summer sun, too—the way it glinted off the oiled bodies of other sunners and warmed the creamy lotion I occasionally put on my own. But for me swimming was primarily an escape from the sun; any tan I had was secondary. I was not tempted to join the girls who lay all afternoon sautéing in the sun, occasionally sizzling their feet in the pool.

With adolescence, everything connected with the body seemed more bothersome. Before you swam you had to shave your legs and underarms; afterward you had to wash your hair. And then there was the host of unpleasant sensations that had always accompanied swimming: ears that, despite vigorous shaking, stayed clogged with water until late evening; water in the nostrils that caused an irritation no sneeze could relieve; rats in the hair that no brush could get through; and eyes that watered all evening from the chlorine. As a child these minor discomforts never kept me out of the pool. But as I grew older, I noticed them more. When a coed church group was deciding whether to go swimming or skating, my first impulse was to vote for swimming; but after some of the girls pointed out these inconveniences, I relented and voted for skating.

Shortly before I entered high school, the YMCA built an indoor swimming pool. Olympic size, with ropes marking off lanes for laps, it looked more professional than any of the other pools in town. I had swum occasionally in a private indoor pool, west of town, called "the Bubble" because of the plastic dome that encased it. Swimming in the winter was a lark. But on a regular basis, it did not appeal to me: no blazing sun, water so clouded with chlorine that the bottom of the pool was obscured, and the bother of having to change clothes and dry my hair there. Swimming did not become a winter pastime.

Once I was in high school, it was barely a summer activity. The summer after my sophomore year I returned to the Big Pool to teach beginning swimmers and to take lifesaving lessons. Looking at the chattering second-graders wrapped in their towels and, beyond them, to the sides of the pool, where leaves collected in the gutter, and at the bottom of the pool, where thick, black globs of tar appeared, I realized that the size and the cold no longer impressed me. The lifesaving lessons were difficult. Since I was the only person in the class, I had to swim the long laps across the pool by myself. The end goal—being a lifeguard—did not seem worth it. Sitting all day above the water in the hot sun, blowing whistles and yelling at kids to stay off the rope, and compiling a wardrobe of swimsuits—what did that have to do with swimming anyway? The next two summers I avoided the pool.

Books, meanwhile, assumed a new authority in my life. Dissatisfied with the social life offered by high school, I let books invade areas of my life previously impermeable. Contemporary nonfiction changed my opinions about feminism, the Vietnam War, and religion. As a child I had sought geographical respite from Kansas through my reading; in high school I sought ideological escape.

Fiction, though, retained the most powerful influence over me. Having rejected teenage love stories wholesale, I turned to serious literature. My selection was somewhat desultory, though favoring the gloomy or cynical. I imagined Hardy's tortured souls on the High Plains rather than on the moors; phrases from Vonnegut—"so it goes"—crept into my conversation; and Sinclair Lewis's exposition of babbittry justified my ridicule of pep clubs and booster organizations.

My thirst for mysteries was quenched by foreign authors. I remember sitting in my attic bedroom inherited from my older sisters, light streaming through the window onto a worn, paperback copy of *Crime and Punishment* lying on an antiqued yellow chest. Though I had never heard of Dostoevsky, I sensed that this book held far greater mysteries than those encountered by Nancy Drew. Now that I was experiencing some dissonance between the everyday world and myself, I wanted to read about the trials of those from other times and places. Books lent me a platform from which to survey the surrounding scene.

A group made up mostly of drama and debate students shared my taste for literature, but between longtime friends and me, it proved a barrier. As children we had acted out the stories we read, borrowing names, situations, and settings and incorporating them with what we knew firsthand. Sometimes I did choose to read rather than play with a friend, but I felt no disjunction between literature and life. Books were the raw material for my life. In high school, though I tried to keep up with the constant stream of activities and gossip, I found that I was more and more out of touch with friends and that we had less and less to talk about. At lunch I would often read a novel to provide relief from the tedious banality of everyday conversations.

"I read too much," is the explanation I sometimes offer to people who ask why I left Kansas. But reading itself has changed since those days. In college it grew solitary and academic, more detached from life, lacking both the escape of my childhood reading and the intensity of my high-school reading. Now demands of the unimagined world distract me. I am more often the fly caught in the web than the spider suspended by it.

If reading led me to leave Kansas, though, visiting there has helped me rekindle my initial love of reading. The sumer I was twenty-five, I took my youngest sister, Megan, age nine, to the library to look up a book I had read at her age. Stuck in the pocket of the book was an old card from the days before the library issued plastic cards to their patrons. On it I found a date from seventeen years before and my name— not once but three times. Separating the signatures were the names of two friends, whom I had apparently coerced into reading and rereading the book. That personal connection, I realized, is when I enjoy reading the most. A friend lends me a book, a sister gives me one, or I overhear my mother talking to a friend about a book that shocked her—these books I am more likely to read than those I collected at book sales during my college days.

That same summer I took Megan swimming at the Big Pool. Several years before, the filter system at the Elks pool had broken down, causing the water to turn a murky green. Eventually it was closed. Weeds grew up around the blue-and-white cinder-block wall, and it was finally converted into a small office building. For a time the Big Pool was also under review, threatened with demolition or costly renovations that might have caused the city to start charging a fee. Instead, citizens and city fathers rallied to support it. Repainted and resurfaced, with a new filter system, diving boards, and a walkway in the shallow end that kids can jump off, the Big Pool was in better condition than when I was growing up. It was also a little more sophisticated: the sign of many adjectives was nowhere in sight. But there was still no charge for admission.

At the end of that summer, watching a city-wide bathtub race from the banks of the Big Pool, I tried to imagine the opening day, sixty years before, when Mayor Trinkle said "Go," and hundreds of people dove in. The Big Pool was the one thing that had not shrunk in Garden City during my absences. I had to grow up to appreciate it. For the first time in seven years, I bought a new swimsuit.

CHAPTER 3

Pomp and Circumstance

I ENJOYED HIGH SCHOOL MOST when I was ten. The brown braid on my oldest sister's marching-band uniform, the bouncing pleats of the brown-and-white pep-club skirt she wore to school every game day, and the sixteenth notes from the first flute part of the Garden City High School Buffalo fight song— all were part of the costuming and score, the pageantry I imagined high school held in store for me. Weekend nights, when Chris let me stay upstairs in her room, we often played a game guessing the names of people in each other's class. When one guessed correctly, the other had to tell everything she knew about the person with that name. This way I learned all about the characters in high school: the boy in band who played the flute with an awful, breathy tone; another boy who fell in love with his English teacher; and the English teacher from the South who always threatened to "turn you over my checkered apron." She never mentioned the cruel things said and done to her by some of the popular girls in her class. High school was a world I looked forward to.

Chris was not a typical teenager of the mid-1960s—not like the girls with long, blond, stringy hair my friends and I saw dancing on *American Bandstand* and *Shindig*. Her hair was short and dark, and she did not spend long hours on the phone or talk in code or beg my parents for the car. After school she worked downtown in the library. Most evenings she sat at the long, narrow desk built into one of the coves of her attic bedroom, writing themes or reading or working trig problems. The only sympton of adolescence in evidence was a bad case of acne, which marred the angelic complexion I admired in her First Communion picture hanging in my parents' bedroom.

Though Chris had no dates in high school, I never caught her mourning over unsent valentines or waiting for the phone to ring. She participated in Kayettes and pep club, played in the band, worked on the yearbook, and attended Girls' State. On the night of prom she went to the banquet before the dance alone, dressed in white gloves and a long dress. From our bedroom just east of the front door, my younger sister and I often heard her come in and would beg her to tell us about her night. Her detailed accounts assured me that, thought not popular, she was happy.

That conclusion was perhaps more a reflection of my own state of unconscious contentment. In fifth grade I was well liked by classmates and teachers, and life seemed full of things intended to please me—friends, piano lessons, cats, books, and swimming. High school would be ever better. I would do all the things that Chris did, only I would be more popular— have more friends, more phone calls, and more invitations to parties. Chris seemed to recognize this ambition. One Halloween as I was getting ready to go trick-or-treating, I remarked with disgust about the teenagers out throwing eggs at cars and spraying shaving cream on bushes. "In a few years you'll be out there with them," she said quietly.

On the night of her graduation, in May, 1967, flanked by all the extended family we could muster—two grandmothers, a grandfather, two great aunts, my parents, and three siblings—I watched the gowned graduates march in, evenly spaced and in time to the stately music played by the band Chris had once been part of. How I would miss the high, clear tone of her flute coming down the stairs from the attic. Around me people fanned themselves with their programs in the hot, close basketball gym, while I scrutinized mine, matching many of the 250 names with the black-and-white photographs I had memorized from the yearbooks.

Chris was named co-valedictorian of her class. She made us proud as she walked across the makeshift stage to receive her diploma. Her name was called again in recognition of a scholarship she had won to a small, private liberal arts college in Florida, twelve hundred miles away. "Tell them how much it's for," said my maternal grandmother, who still harbored a trace of the accent she had brought from Germany as a child. "No," my parents hushed, afraid that those sitting around us had heard and knowing that even with the scholarship they would have a difficult time affording the school. I sided with my grandmother.

The invited speaker, a professor of education, talked about campus protests. If any of the graduates felt they must participate, they should make it constructive rather than destructive, he advised them. Three years later at her college graduation, Chris would wear a black armband in protest of the Vietnam War; but at that moment during her high-school graduation, I wondered only what we would do with her green cup in the kitchen cabinet when she left home next fall.

After the ceremony I fondled the tassel on her cap longingly and asked if I could have it. "No," she said firmly, refusing me for one of the few times I can remember. "You'll get one of your own when you graduate."

Two years later, braving an angry-looking thunderhead and a tornado watch, we watched my second sister graduate. A stormy close to a stormy three years.

What I knew of Nancy during those years came more from observation than from what she told me. She washed her hair in beer and used the cans as rollers. Rumpled clothes and dirty breakfast dishes covered the floor of the attic bedroom. The phone was often busy, and the family car was often gone. And she was always late—going to school or church or lessons and getting home again. An early morning call at our house meant that she had missed the bus for a school orchestra trip; a late night call meant that she had missed the pep-club bus after a football game in Dodge City.

In some ways I was proud that she cared more about clothes and boys than Chris did, that there were antics I could tell my friends about. At night, from my bedroom window, I watched her and her boyfriend kiss on the front porch, and when she wasn't home I read the notes scrawled in her yearbooks. But I resented the inconvenience, the disruption of routine she caused: making me late for music lessons when she kept the car out too long and making my mother worried and red-eyed much of the time. The frequent cross fire of angry words and accusations made me vow never to cause my parents as much trouble as she had.

Nancy's temperament had been established long before. Shortly after her birth, she is said to have upstaged Chris, the firstborn and first grandchild on one side of the family. An early Christmas picture showing her with eyes sparkling and fists clenched with excitement suggests something of the fireball she was and the ball of fury she would become. Though less patient and steady than Chris, Nancy was more inventive and imaginative. With a neighbor friend and me she played the hunched-over witch from Hansel and Gretel, told us ghost stories, and made little books with drawings and stories about cats that we could hold in the palms of our hands.

In high school she had less time for a meddling sister and her tag-along friends. She participated in dramatics and spent long hours after school rehearsing for plays, often missing the supper my mother reheated for her. A glamorous life it seemed to me: frantic searches of the house for props; last-minute costume stitching; thick, bright makeup; the glow of the stage lights in the dark, crowded auditorium on opening night; and all-night cast parties. I could hardly wait for my own debut.

Yet it was when Nancy was rehearsing for something in dramatics that I often felt a keen sense of rejection or separation from her. She became angry when I pulled off the red bandanna she was using as a blindfold to prepare for the Helen Keller tryouts. Another time, as I sat by the old gas stove in her bedroom, she let me hold her script for *The Lark* while she recited the lines, and I noticed that she spoke with a British-sounding accent instead of the normal Kansas twang. This malleability of voice and attitude made me uneasy. I wasn't sure who my sister was anymore.

Nancy was not the typical teenager I had envisioned. In eighth grade, at Saint Mary's, she had been a cheerleader, but at the public high school she was not, nor did she want to be. Nancy didn't seem to care what other people thought: she went to the prom with a boy, but without shoes; she spoke critically of certain classmates, teachers, and administrators, often getting into arguments in class; and she went out with a boy my parents disapproved of. I didn't know much about the revolution going on in the world around Garden City in 1969 or about the content of my sister's complaints, but I sensed in her challenge to authority and convention a strong indictment of what my family believed and the way we lived.

On the other hand, I was trying desperately to belong to a group and conform to its standards. Seventh grade had jolted me into adolescence. At Saint Mary's girls had to wear uniforms—an attempt, I suppose, to establish some sort of social and economic equality. But the polarization of popular and unpopular girls was sharper that year than in years when we were allowed to wear regular clothes, dictating where a girl sat in a classroom and who she ate with at lunch. I was caught in between, liking some of the girls deemed unpopular but wanting desperately to be one of the elite. I felt caught, too, between pleasing the girls I wanted to be like and pleasing teachers. Intelligence had become a handicap in the race for popularity. I found myself apologizing for knowing answers to questions asked in class. I could no longer rely on my instincts—what I thought, felt, and preferred—to help me make or keep friends. Toward the end of the year I became fed up with pretending to like things I didn't and joined the unpopular girls on the other side of the room.

Once that year, when I was still in the competition, Nancy saw me hang up the phone in tears. She came over and hugged me. She knew what it was like to feel you had no friends, she told me. Her gesture surprised me: she seemed to have lots of friends. More often, though, the breach in ages and temperaments and my own stern disapproval of the disruptions she caused kept us apart and unaware of the similarity of our feelings.

Few details of Nancy's graduation have stayed with me. Two students, the Outstanding Girl and Boy selected by the senior class, gave the speeches, but the audience in the football stadium seemed more intent on watching the ominous clouds above. Nancy graduated with honors without effort. Our Grandmother Hope lay dying in the hospital a few blocks away. Of all our relatives, she was the one Nancy resembled most physically—under five foot tall, with a full bosom, baby-fine hair, and thick-lensed, wire-rimmed glasses—but perhaps the least temperamentally, my grandmother being a perfectionist with a tightly corseted regard for convention.

Most parents left immediately after their child had shaken the appropriate hands and received a diploma, relieved to get out from under the threatening skies. Three months later, with a similar relief, I would watch Nancy leave home, my grip a little slackened, but still holding onto my dreams of high school.

The year of my brother's graduation, 1972, was dominated by one issue: the dress code, which meant no long hair for boys and no jeans for girls. In the name of preventing classroom disruption, administrators stood in the cafeteria and halls, taking down names of boys whose hair crept over their collars and then calling them out of their classes over the intercom. Girls who wore pants of blue denim with outside seams, back pockets, and back yokes (the official definition of jeans) were snagged in hallways and given passes to go home and change.

The dress code seemed to be the administration's attempt to hold at bay the eruptions of youth taking place elsewhere in the country. But it served as a rallying point for the class of 1972. They mobilized the student council, using the meetings to discuss strategies for changing school policy rather than homecoming centerpieces. By the end of the year the dress code was changed, though too late to benefit them.

Quentin was a part of this struggle. He wore his hair long and coedited an underground newspaper for an American government project. He also succeeded at traditional things—winning debate tournaments, starring in school plays, and serving as junior-class president. During his senior year when he was asked to give a speech at a men's club downtown, he spoke frankly but not bitterly about the high school's main problem: boredom. At seventeen, Quentin was already a diplomat, a negotiator—more than the high-school administrators, who could be set into a tailspin by the slightest sign of disagreement.

At commencement ceremonies that year, the Outstanding Senior Boy did not gloss over the conflicts in graduation clichés. "I do not feel achievement—I feel defeated. I do not feel happy—I feel relieved," he said in his speech that night. Comparing the extracurricular concerns of his classmates—marriage, jobs, college—with the restrictions placed on them in high school, he charged, "When we went back to school it was like leaving the real world and falling asleep." His classmates gave him a standing ovation. The dress-code victory did not go unrecognized either. One of the last graduates to cross the stage grabbed the wig he had worn all year long and flung it into the air, his long hair unfolding in the wind.

The program gave evidence of grade inflation: almost seventy students—more than a fifth of the class—were listed as graduating with honors or high honors. Quentin was salutatorian; another boy was valedictorian. When the latter became Garden City's first Rhodes Scholar years later, one of the high-school administrators would not be able to recall anything outstanding about him: "He was never in athletics or anything."

During the ceremony I sat with the band below the stage on the football field, wearing the faded, worn uniform that had seemed so regal a few years before and playing the endless series of *legato* notes on the beat. Earlier in the year I had discovered that if you were a clarinet or flute or any other woodwind, it really didn't matter what you played on the marching field because you were always blasted out by the drums and trumpets. And usually your fingers were too numb with cold even to move, much less scamper over all the trills and grace notes Sousa delighted in. Staying in step was all that mattered.

I had started my first year of high school with high hopes. During my eighth- and ninth-grade years at the public junior high school, I had made friends with a group of girls who were neither particularly popular nor unpopular. The day we received our sophomore schedules, we walked all over the large T-shaped building to determine if we could make it to all of our classes in the allotted six minutes. Our lockers were located next to one another on the second floor of the main building, a convenience arranged by one girl's mother who worked at the high school. During the day we would meet there to discuss weekend plans and exchange confidences. After school I walked home with three or four of the girls who lived southeast of the high school. Later in the year, as some of the girls turned sixteen, I sometimes rode home with them, always by way of the Main drag: an L-shaped trek down Main and Fulton, with Stevens Park and the Creamee Drive-in as the turnaround points.

With these friends I participated in pep club, Kayettes, and band. Other activities, though, particularly drama and debate, drew me into contact with juniors and seniors, many of them friends of my brother. They were a more seasoned, cynical bunch than my friends from junior high. I enjoyed their sarcasm and their play with ideas and words—even when I was not familiar with the subject. Having often read a *Mad* satire of a movie without having seen the film, I could easily pick up the cadence of their humor.

That atmosphere made me more attuned to the absurdities of high school: the helicopter hired to hover over the football field and dry it out for the state play-offs; the emergency pep-club meeting in the middle of sixth hour (called by the basketball coach to chastise the girls for not doing their part in supporting his losing team); and the arbitrary censoring of the school play, *Auntie Mame,* by the administrators the night before the opening show. Even as the graduates crossed the stage, the girl sitting next to me pointed out the girls that her brother had had sex with, and one of the administrators stumbled over the name of the foreign-exchange student who had been there all year.

Though the dominant cast of my mind was becoming negative, I was not yet disheartened. The class of 1972 had fought back, and the graduation had been a good show of solidarity, I felt. I had read Upton Sinclair's *The Jungle* and felt something akin to the feverish burst of socialism at the end. The oppressed versus their oppressors—that was a team I could cheer for.

"Grandma, I'm stuck in Garden City." The words, blurted into a pay phone, carried through the open door of the Trailways bus station as a friend and I walked by one summer day. The speaker, a boy of about twelve with a mud-colored cowlick pointing out from his thin head, looked as if he had never been any place much better. But my friend and I knew the feeling.

Bus trips were our means of escape in those days, though they were mostly just to high-school debate tournaments in other small western Kansas towns—Satanta, Hoxie, Liberal, and Ulysses. Occasionally we traveled as far east as El Dorado, Winfield, Ark City, or Emporia (for the Tournament of Silver and Roses). Our junior year my friend and I had become the top debate team, by default, when the other experienced debators dropped out and the counselors filled the novice classes with people who could not distinguish a premise from a conclusion. On long stretches of two-lane highway, we made up wild counterplans, documented by absurd sources, and placed them in classrooms for other, humorless debate teams to find. Riding back home late at night, we sang old protest songs we had memorized from the scratched records of older brothers and sisters.

If boredom had been the only problem, I could have passed through high school and my last years in Garden City relatively unscathed. But things there seemed not only lifeless, but twisted. A sense of betrayal and outrage dominated my last two years of high school.

The extracurricular activities I had looked forward to as a child proved disappointing. Fewer, less ambitious plays were produced. The drama crowd dwindled as people graduated early or lost interest because of conflicts with the director. No one came to the performances. My senior year I looked forward to the formation of a symphonic wind ensemble, but we sent out for doughnuts almost as much as we played. Pep club no longer interested me, as I felt sports was the one activity that already received too much attention.

Occasionally I tried to challenge that mentality. One day in my trigonometry class the teacher, a football coach, announced that we were going to see an "educational" film. It was about the Green Bay Packers. The next hour my government teacher—another football coach—smiled slyly and said that we would be seeing a film in class the next day. When I went to an administrator to complain, he said that he understood my concern but was not sure he could do anything about it at this point. I felt vindicated the next day when the football coach in my government class announced with a red face that he could not show the film because some parents had called in and complained. Several weeks later, though, the football coach/trigonometry teacher showed another football film in class. "Sit down and shut up," he told me when I walked in. "If you don't want to watch it, then just turn your desk around."

Classes with teachers who were not coaches were not much better. Nearing her retirement, the English teacher with the checkered apron had given up teaching and settled for sighs of "Y'all will never make it through college." In the name of innovation, core courses in English, biology, and history had been divided up into nine-week minicourses. My year of American history consisted of four minicourses, all about the twentieth century, none in chronological order—as if the burden of the past could be eased by chopping it up into independent, digestible units and then scrambling them. During one of those classes—in 1973—my history teacher spoke of

the Vietnam War in the past perfect. A few people had pro-
tested, he said, but the majority of the American people had
supported the government's efforts in Vietnam.

A similar disregard for the history of the high school had
struck my class. With the class of 1972 graduated and the
dress code amended, protest gave way to pranks. Random
acts of vandalism—setting lavatory trash cans on fire and
riding motorcycles through the hallways—became the primary
means of expression. Boys who in other years might have been
class leaders stole the Spirit Trophy and revived the art of
mooning. The National Merit Finalist came to the prom drunk
and dressed in overalls. The football team shoplifted during an
out-of-town trip. Apathy was the byword of my class.

Occasionally I tried to join in this spirit, or lack of spirit. I
boycotted pep rallies, suggested "You're So Vain" as the
theme song for the prom my class planned, and went stag—
dressed in tennis shoes and a long skirt that I borrowed from
my mother—to my senior prom. But these acts were viewed
more as iconoclasm than apathy, and they met with a cool
reception from most of my classmates.

When I took on more serious matters in classes, I met with
open hostility. I made a few reverberations in that small
pond—enough to label me as "smart" in some eyes and a
"smart aleck" in the eyes of others. The same prejudices and
pettiness that had slighted Chris and angered Nancy frustrated
me. I did not want to be quiet and stoic like Chris or emotional
and explosive like Nancy. I wanted to strike the note of reason,
to fight it out with logic and sense. But it was too lonely. There
was a cause, it seemed, but no other rebels.

Times had changed. The spirit of protest that had united my
brother's class two years later divided me from mine. I had
fallen out of step—become an anachronism. My younger sister Rosemary would call me a child of the 1960s. But when I
went away to college the next year, I found that things had
been taken care of. Nixon resigned in August of my freshman
year; the troops came home in the spring. Protest graffitti
scrawled on sidewalks and bathroom walls appeared as ancient
and indecipherable as hieroglyphics.

I wore no tassel for my graduation, having escaped my class at the first opportunity by graduating in January. In May, though, I returned as an observer, sitting in the stadium with the parents and siblings of my classmates. My father and two younger sisters stayed home; my mother handed out diplomas with the other school-board members. Until that moment I had not realized the awkwardness my decision not to participate would cause her.

Twenty percent of the class graduated with some kind of honors, though the program did not list the names. No salutatorian or valedictorian was named, the titles having been abolished. One speech, given by the person I credited with having turned the student council back into a homecoming committee, started out, "Life is like an Oreo cookie. . . ." The wind caused the microphone to crackle, however, and I never heard the simile explained.

In the years since high school, in other places, I have encountered many of the same things that bothered me then— the ineffectuality and pettiness of administrators, stubborn adherence to meaningless traditions, and a shrinking from passion and thought—but never in such a concentrated form. Sitting in the stadium that night, wind tangling my hair, I didn't know how to tell my parents that what looked like an act of family disloyalty was actually an expression of allegiance to them. Memories of other high-school years, other graduations, would not let me pretend that this ceremony was anything more than a bad end to my years in Garden City.

CHAPTER 4

Salmagundi

FOR AS LONG AS I CAN REMEMBER, my mother has spent her Wednesday afternoons, October through March, at Salmagundi. Started in 1901 by a doctor's wife who did not intend to give up the finer things in life when they moved to the High Plains from Saint Louis, Salmagundi is the oldest women's club in Garden City and one of the few "uplift" clubs to which my mother has ever belonged. Soap operas, women's magazines, weekly hair appointments, and other things strictly female, she always shunned. Salmagundi was her one exception.

During spring break of my last year of college, I accompanied my mother to a Salmagundi meeting. A few years earlier, having spurned things labeled "female only," I probably would have refused her offer. But it had become something of a family tradition: my two older sisters had each made a visit at my age. And I was curious to see where she had been spending her Wednesday afternoons.

The name "Salmagundi" fascinated me as a child—how much more exotic it sounded than "PTO" or "Altar Society." Specifically it refers to a salad, with rows of chopped meats, anchovies, eggs, and vegetables arranged for contrast. The club, though, refers to the more general meaning: a potpourri, a mixture of unlike ingredients. An apt name for women who spend much of their lives mixing the miscellaneous, the available to come up with palatable concoctions.

My own experience with cooking and clubs started in fifth grade, when I joined the Eager Beavers 4-H Club. The unchallenged, hierarchical structure of 4-H was familiar to me from Catholic school; but joining as late in the year as I did was like entering parochial school after everyone else had memorized the Baltimore Catechism, received their first Communion, and been confirmed. During that first meeting—my first glimpse of parliamentary procedure—the round of reports and the motioning and seconding seemed as foreign to me as all the kneeling, standing, and sitting at Masses must have seemed to my Protestant friend who had talked me into joining. The elaborate record keeping required reminded me of the score keeping necessary for Confession. "How often do you wash your curtains?" I was asked when I took Room Improvement. "Your windows? Your walls?" My mother filled out that form. Cooking was easier—I only had to keep track of the meals I fixed.

Though I followed the 4-H sequence of cooking—"Snacks and Little Lunches," "Lunches and Dinners," "Picnics and Suppers"—I was spared much knowledge of cooking. I cooked by reading recipes and the sides of cans and boxes, not by understanding the various ingredients and how they interact with one another. Cooking for me was a special event and not an everyday task. If I lacked an ingredient, I sped off to the store rather than searching the cupboard for an available substitute. I learned to make individual items (popcorn, orange juice from a concentrate, Waldorf salad, and cookies), to prepare isolated meals, and the proper order in which to wash dishes (even though my family owned a dishwasher). But nothing of spices or leftovers or timing.

Judgment day came with the county fair. Uniformity seemed to be the prized virtue—Were your loaves perfectly rounded, your cookies the same size and shade of doneness? An electric knife, my mother and I discovered, cut a roll of refrigerator cookie dough into identical, wafer-thin pieces. I preferred drop cookies with lumps of chocolate chips or raisins, but the delicate refrigerator cookies won the purple ribbon and a trip to the state fair. My growing skepticism about the whole process was confirmed one year when a fellow Eager Beaver won a purple ribbon for a box mix cake. Her mother had been in the hospital during the fair, and, not knowing there was any other way to make a cake, the girl had pulled a box off the shelf and mixed it up.

My mother had had her own victory with a box cake when she was first married. Invited to a covered-dish supper, she was a little nervous, knowing that several farm women, veteran scratch cooks, would be there. Box cakes had just come out on the market, though, and always one for domestic conveniences, my mother tried one. The farm ladies loved it and asked for her recipe.

Such stories from the home front made my awkwardness at learning the domestic arts somewhat easier to bear. Catholic schooling hinted that I was not a holy female, 4-H that I was not wholly female. I failed as a potential nun because I lacked the sine qua non: a high, thin, clear singing voice; a consistently neat, effortless script; and regular attendance at Saturday Mass. I failed as an Eager Beaver homemaker because when I sewed, I ripped out as much as I stitched; when I made a poster for a demonstration talk, the letters were crooked and smudged; and when I peeled a potato, I ended up with a small ball of spud and a bleeding thumb. At the end of my fourth year in 4-H, I dropped out, still feeling unqualified for ordination into this predominantly female priesthood.

The year before, in eighth grade, I had been one of a thimbleful of girls in school who did not take home economics. My older sisters had not taken it, and I had the impression from my family that it was not a proper school subject. A friend warned that I would never be a good housewife and mother. Nonsense, my mother told me. She had never taken it. Days when smells of cookies or cakes drifted out into the hallway as I was going to my Spanish class, I sometimes regretted my decision. I was left out of many conversations and activities, FHA—Future Homemakers of America—being the most popular girls' organization in junior high. But I was relieved not to have to take sewing, and the next year when I saw my friends planning their honeymoons and dreamhouses for class, I felt no envy. Those didn't seem to me like things you planned. At least not at age fourteen.

Part of my rejection of domesticity at that age was defensiveness: I felt I was not good at it, and to cover my ineptitude, I feigned indifference. But part of it, too, stemmed from a fear of being hemmed into a life that I didn't want. A girl was either domestic or she wasn't, as I saw it. She either grew up, married, had children, and spent the rest of her life cooking, cleaning, and washing, or she grew up and did other things.

What those other things were, I wasn't sure. I had no clear image to replace the homemaker with. Though my sixth-grade teacher had once called me a tomboy, I never considered myself one. I wasn't particularly athletic: I dreaded gym class as much as I would have dreaded home ec. And tests indicated that my mechanical aptitude was far below normal.

In other respects, though, I considered myself a normal girl. My sophomore year I spent much time and effort on my appearance. I wore contacts, makeup, a dress, hose, and heels to school amost every day. Again, though, these were things that did not come quite naturally. They seemed doomed to failure. By midyear I had to stop wearing the contacts because of an ulcer in my eye, perhaps caused by the eye makeup I was wearing. Hose ran and snagged; heels hurt my feet. At the end of the year, when the dress code changed, I started wearing jeans and T-shirts every day and stopped wearing makeup.

More comfortable and less expensive and time-consuming, my asexual uniform was in many ways liberating. I never thought twice about what to put on in the morning, and I never had to change clothes after school or watch how I sat (particularly important in that era of the miniskirt). At times, though, it was constricting. If ever I wore anything different—even just a shirt other than a T-shirt—it was sure to provoke comment.

It wasn't that I wanted to be a boy. Once when I was changing clothes for a play rehearsal, a girl laughed and said I took off my shirt "like a boy." What did that mean? I was a girl, I had always been a girl. I had never wanted to be anything else but a girl. Wasn't anything I did, by definition, "like a *girl*"?

In high school, though, I learned to distrust that phrase "like a girl." Sometimes it was used to prescribe a certain kind of behavior. One day when I wore my good purple dress—my debate dress—to science class, a girl commented on how nice I looked. "She may be dressed like a girl, but she doesn't act like a girl," said the male teacher. He was referring to my sharp tongue. In other classes I heard echoes of that message: good girls wear dresses and keep their mouths shut. Other times the phrase was used derogatorily, like a diminutive. When the school literary magazine came out, another male teacher said that a poem of mine was obviously written "by a girl."

Smart-mouthed, irresponsible, sullen, lazy—any of these epithets could have been applied accurately to me at one time or another in high school. Instead, though, I was always attacked because of my sex, faulted both for having its characteristics and for not having them. My clothes thus became more than mere preference; they were a statement, a way of dissociating myself from what I had come to see as "trappings"—not the means by which to "trap" a male, but the means by which to trap oneself. If being "nice" and "pretty" meant forfeiting your mind and spirit, then I chose to keep mine and risk being labeled unfeminine.

In college, defined more by my academic ability than by my domesticity or appearance, I was less conscious of being female. What I thought was more important than what I wore. I could cook a meal or sew on a button without feeling that it endangered my integrity or future. Even so, the thought of spending an afternoon with housewives and mothers at Salmagundi made me a little nervous. Would my old feelings of inadequacy return? Or would I act superior?

Upon entering the house of the hostess of the week I felt a momentary panic as I looked around the color-coordinated living room. *House Beautiful*. The hostess had done all the decorating, as well as the landscaping outside, my mother murmured to me. I nodded.

A friendly rumble of laughter and gentle banter ascended from below as my mother led the way down softly carpeted stairs into a room of oranges and yellows radiating warmth. We chose seats near a sun-streamed window. Above my head hung a planter of Swedish Ivy, voluptuous and vibrant. I thought of the limp, yellow ivy that hung in my dorm room.

Other women came into the room, some in slacks, others in dresses, all with an air of at-home casualness. I recognized most of them. Many had attended college, and several held degrees. All had married and reared children. My mother pointed out a few of the new, younger women, one of whom was a lawyer who had never practiced law.

Sitting in this room of women, I was reminded of the days of my paper-doll villages, populated with models cut out from Sears and Roebuck catalogues and store-bought Lennon sister paper dolls discarded by my older sisters. Because few full-length male models appeared in the catalogues, virtually all my families were headed by women. Most of them had lots of children—I liked the cute cartoon babies in the catalogue. I gave Peggy Lennon, who was dressed in a strapless blue swimsuit, five or six toddlers of about the same age. At least once a day I spread out all the families into neighborhoods around the braided rug in the dining room and constructed elaborate scenarios that included every doll. The absence of men did not strike me as strange at the time, probably because the fathers I knew in real life did not figure in the day-to-day activities of mothers and children. Now as I looked around the room, I tried to think of these women's husbands. None of them, I realized, had made a distinct impression on me, as many of these women had.

The hostess had attended college with my mother, where she excelled in math and met her husband. She had a degree in engineering, though she had never held a paying job in that capacity. In three years she had had four children, including a set of twins, followed thirteen years later by a fifth child. While her husband advanced from schoolteacher to high-school principal to superintendent to president of the local community college, she taught math at the high-school and college levels, sewed clothes for her children, decorated several houses, typed her husband's dissertation, and—more reluctantly—cooked. Her homemade Christmas gifts to our home often came accompanied by clever poems.

To my right sat my high-school English teacher, who had retired before my senior year of high school. She looked rested and ten years younger. White hair puffed around her head, and she talked and laughed freely. In the classroom she had been harried and flighty. Her husband had died many years before, and she had reared her two daughters alone, supporting them by teaching Shakespeare to indifferent teenagers. After she retired, she and a friend had gone to Europe. My mother had told me that they were without luggage for ten days, a situation that would unnerve many women my age, I knew. They laughed it off, though, bought new toothbrushes, and continued as planned.

My own mother gave up a promising career as a journalist and married my father, bearing him six children and seeing him through law school and political campaigns. After her third child, my brother, was born, the editor of the Garden City paper offered her a regular column. Three times a week was what he had in mind, but since he paid by the column, she raised it to six. We needed the money was her explanation. Putting a price tag on it seemed to help her justify the time not strictly devoted to family or community.

These women exemplified my mother's dictum that women can do whatever they have to do. Their lives had taken unexpected twists and turns as their own ambitions and plans were superceded by the needs and desires of others. And yet they were gracious, versatile, and lively in a way in which their husbands, who pursued their own careers and goals, were not. They had spent much of their lives in the kitchen, but they were not circumscribed by it.

As the president called the meeting to order, the conversations around me dwindled. The business portion was short and informal, necessities dismissed efficiently with a flair. For the program a woman I recognized from my childhood reviewed a book about the lives of several women, including Carry Nation and Amelia Earhart—both unconventional women from Kansas, one who did what she felt she had to do, and one who did what she wanted.

At refreshment time, as my mother and several other women rose to help the hostess, several women turned to me and asked about my plans after graduation.

"Graduate school," I said firmly. "I want to teach college English." Glancing at my high-school English teacher, I added, as if by way of apology, that I had considered teaching high-school English.

"Oh, for heaven's sake, go on to school," she said. "Stay away from teaching high school. You wouldn't like it."

She was right. Teaching high-school English, especially in Garden City or anywhere in western Kansas, would have felt like failure to me. My tenuous adult self needed a greater psychological and geographical distance from the scene of my painful adolescence. There were still people in town that I avoided seeing because of slights or misunderstandings from years before.

Envisioning my life away from Garden City, though, was more difficult than I had anticipated. A few weeks earlier I had interviewed for a graduate fellowship. The interviewer, from the East, seemed amused by my rural background. He made me feel quaint. I did not balk, though, until he asked me what I wanted to be doing in ten years. Ten years? Ten years ago I had been eleven—how different life had looked then. What would it look like ten years from now? Where would I be living? Who would I be living with? What would I be like? He was waiting for a career objective, but I did not feel easy making such projections. How often do you wash your walls? Dream houses had been replaced with dream careers. I felt rushed. Didn't life just happen to you, I wanted to ask the women sitting around me. Don't you deal with things as they come up? Would you have been able to answer that question?

In part, my failure of imagination stemmed from my observation that many of the best things in life were unplanned. The summer before my senior year of high school, after a twelve-year hiatus, my mother had given birth to another girl. The event caused a stir among my parents' friends, many of whom were already grandparents. Certainly it altered any plans my mother had for how she would spend her next eighteen years, but I never saw her waver for an instant. From the attic storeroom she retrieved the bassinet that had made the rounds of many friends and acquaintances, converted my brother's room into a nursery, drank milk, and walked a mile daily. Shortly after she delivered she was sitting up in her hospital bed greeting friends and well-wishers. I had never seen her look so pretty, dressed in a light-blue robe, her brown eyes shining, her cheeks flushed.

The baby was another matter. She seemed like a colorless blob of clay. I was nervous holding her at first—her head flopped back like that of a rag doll if I did not steady it with my hand. Gradually, with each yawn and warble and smile, Megan became a person. During that year when so many absolutes dissolved for me, she was my one saving grace. Nothing hindered or impeded the flow of good will and pleasure that I felt in her existence. As the oldest child at home then (one other sister, four-and-a-half years younger, was also home), I willingly and happily assumed care of her. I was not ready to have a child of my own, certainly—being a teenage mother, wed or unwed, was the bleakest existence I could imagine. But her arrival did make leaving home difficult.

In the years since that afternoon at Salmagundi, I have begun to take a greater interest in what the women I grew up with are doing. I had ignored their wedding invitations, threatening to come dressed in black. Those who knew me best did not bother even to send an invitation. In recent years, though, we have gotten together occasionally on my visits home. Most of them seem content. One kept jogging and played in a racquetball tournament while pregnant. Another looked right at home wiping mustard off the face of her child while her bandanna slipped off her head. Their lives will be much like those of their mothers. At times I envy them their friendly, familiar world. They will travel far in Garden City.

I feel a greater kinship, though, with those women for whom Garden City did not have much to offer. Their dreams

led them to traverse greater distances. One of my former debate partners is singing opera in Europe, and another friend,
in a doctoral program in parasitology, hopes to go to Africa.
My two older sisters have gone east, one to the North to be a
medical doctor, and one to the South to work as a doctor of
sociology. Our paths have been less certain, more solitary.
There is a sense of discontinuity between our lives in Garden
City and our lives now.

In terms of domestic habits, my sisters and I qualify as "career women," according to my mother. We don't wash curtains
or dust the tops of picture frames. Since graduate school I have
not lived any place long enough to feel it necessary to wash
the walls, except to get back a cleaning deposit. Cleaning for
me is an occasional event, prompted by company, procrasti-
nation, or a need for order in my life. Clean window sills are
a sign that I am avoiding something else that needs to be done.

But I have developed some enthusiasm for cooking. Scrub-
bing vegetables, figuring out what to do with a cup of leftover
rice, and experimenting with spices are small tasks that I enjoy. All the senses are involved in cooking: listening for the
water in a covered pot to bubble before adding the spaghetti,
watching corn-on-the-cob brighten in a pot of boiling water,
pinching a peach to test for ripeness, smelling a leftover warm-
ing up in the oven, and tasting a sauce while it's simmering.
My own preference, though, is for a slumgullion rather than a
salmagundi—a stew with a similar variety of ingredients but
requiring less attention to arrangement.

The women of my generation are experimenting with diets,
trying to balance the staples: duty and desire. Some have gone
for the whole buffet—motherhood, career, and an active social
life—and have come away stuffed, not fully digesting any of
the courses. Some combine the ingredients into a delicately
balanced and timed soufflé, which the slightest disruption will
collapse. Others have tried single-dish lives of demanding careers, but find themselves cheating between meals—furtively
embroidering on coffee breaks or looking longingly at children
on playgrounds. We trade recipes. Whether it be meals or
lives, we want to know how to coordinate courses, how to

salvage a baking disaster, and how to substitute one item for another.

In the past several years I have heard some of my mother's friends rethink their pasts. If they were young now, they say, they would have a career first and get married later. I remember my own mother typing in the pantry next to the kitchen, where laundry tumbled in the dryer and a casserole baked in the oven. Now that all but one of her children are away, she has moved to the basement to write her columns, away from the phone and the kitchen. It is an exile she has longed for. I ask her, would she choose differently if she had it to do over. No, she likes staying home. But she does not act as a proponent for that kind of life for her daughters.

Each generation turns its regrets into hopes for the next generation, I suppose. Already the temptation to add ingredients to the lives of those younger than I am is strong. I encourage my youngest sister to try things I was afraid of, to consider paths I never did. For her ninth birthday I bought her a student microscope—an instrument I avoided in high school and college, thereby shutting myself off from a way of seeing the world. She uses it. But she also told my mother recently that when she grows up, unlike her older sisters, she wants to have an ironing board—if they are still being made.

The desire is traditional, but the tone conditional. She speaks in terms of the possible. I watch her gathering ingredients from the world around her—composing songs with hymnlike lyrics on the piano, playing her own version of basketball, making up and performing skits with her stuffed animals, joining in discussions with my father about the latest historical society meeting, and doing cartwheels across the lawn. She also cleans and reorganizes her room with a vengeance. For her there is no stigma attached to housework—or anything else, it seems. As she approaches adolescence, I worry that her enthusiasm will be squelched by unimaginative teachers and classmates, that she will be fed monotonous, colorless fare, or find that she often has to eat alone. If I could wish one thing for her in ten years, it would be that she finds a life with both the variety and the camaraderie of Salmagundi.

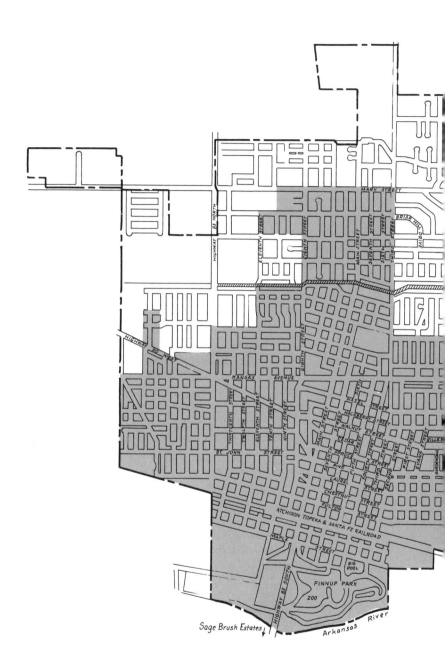

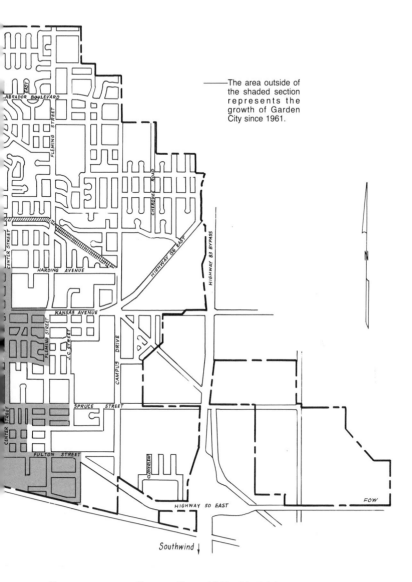

The area outside of the shaded section represents the growth of Garden City since 1961.

DEVELOPMENT OF GARDEN CITY, 1961–86. With the boom in irrigated agriculture, the town grew dramatically between 1961 and 1986. Center Street, which once lay on the eastern edge of town, became more centrally located. (After map prepared by Garden City Area Chamber of Commerce)

CHAPTER 5

Developments

THE FIRST SEVENTEEN YEARS OF MY LIFE I lived in one town, on one street, in one house. That steadiness of location provided me with a sense of stability and continuity. The town did grow and change—new houses were built, old ones torn down, businesses started up and closed—but the changes were gradual and on a scale easily assimilable for a child, and perhaps a bit boring for an adolescent.

The cream-colored two-story house that my family lived in was built in 1908, making it an old house for western Kansas. During my childhood it underwent several changes: the front-porch screen was removed to prevent miller moths from collecting in the bulges, the radiators and gas heating stove were replaced with central heating, two of the three doors leading to my parents' bedroom were removed to allow them more privacy, and their walk-in closet was converted into a half-bath. Despite this modernization, the house retains a strong connection with the past: cats still birth their kittens in the cool dark under the porch, a sister still rocks on the front-porch swing, and my father sleeps in the bedroom in which he was born.

His family were not the original inhabitants. A message in slightly jumbled Latin—"Rex est bonus puer"—and a list of names scrawled in chalk on the furnace-room wall let my siblings and me know that others had lived there before us. Farther back in the basement we found some curious concrete steps leading up to the ceiling. An old outdoor entrance, my father once told me, but I preferred to believe that there were hidden treasures and secret panels involved somehow. On the second floor, in one of the storerooms, I liked to tug at the cotton that wreathed the old coal-stove chimney that poked through the angled ceiling. Santa Claus's beard, my siblings and I insisted. These remnants of another time and family fascinated me as a child and provide some comfort as an adult. Though a house may outlast its inhabitants, it can also stand as a sort of memorial to them. When I move into hospital-clean apartments now, I am disappointed that no vestiges remain of the former residents, no witness to their stay there— no matter how brief.

My family's house is located on what was once the east edge of town, on Gillespie Place, an east-west street only one block long (so that for years the distinction between street and block was not clear to me—I thought all streets were one block long, or that each block had its own name). Not a cul-de-sac, mind you, but more an arbitrary pathway between the busier streets at either end—Evans to the west, and Center to the east. Plats at the Finney County Historical Museum show that originally a continuation of Walnut Street, less than a block over, had been planned, which would have connected Evans and Center and provided a straight shot from Main Street, through the seven number streets and Evans, to Center. Had the construction been carried out, no one but delivery persons, visitors, residents, and the curious would have had any reason to drive down Gillespie. As it was, not many people did use it, mainly Sunday drivers—people who drove by slowly and stared— and teenagers who parked by the field on the southwest end of the street at night to neck. Red brick pillars announcing "Gillespie Place, Private Drive" have always marked the entrance at either end—an attempt to establish a smalltown aristocracy at one time, I suppose. I made the best of it I could, telling friends from other neighborhoods that at one time there had been gates and guards—a story my parents would have discouraged had they known about it.

When I was growing up, there were eleven houses on the

block—eight across the street from us, and three on our side. The oldest and largest house, built in the first few years of the twentieth century, was originally the home of the people after whom Gillespie was named. When a family with children my age moved in, I finally was able to see the second floor: a huge, empty room with a wood floor and slanted ceiling. My father told me it was originally intended as a ballroom; my friends and I used it to learn to skateboard. The other houses on the block established themselves slowly over the years. The last two—brick and one-story—were built in the late 1940s and early 1950s. I always considered them the new houses— though they were older than I was. Located next to one another, in the center of the block, they created a gap in the canopy of trees that lined either side.

The occupations and incomes of the people living on the street varied. They ran a drugstore and a feedyard, sold cars and legal knowledge, set broken arms, and raised Arabian stallions. One family was wealthy; several were retired, reaping the benefits of a life spent working in one place at one thing for a long time. Some of the neighbors my parents had known from other times in their lives: the mother of the family next door had been my mother's college hallmate; in one of the new houses across the street was the father of one of my father's childhood friends. Other neighbors we knew less well, but well enough to include in block parties. The houses were referred to by the names of their inhabitants—even after their namesakes had died or moved away. If a family with children moved in, though, the house was usually rechristened.

Kids had the reign of the neighborhood. Mornings my neighbor and I would beg the milkman for popsicles; afternoons we would beg the mailman for rides on his cart. We trod the low chalk wall that wound around the ivy-covered, orange house at the end of the block, forded the tiny irrigation ditch used to water a garden, and acted out fairytales in the "forest" behind. Young entrepreneurs, we held cardboard-table sales on the busier street of Center, marketing everything from watered-down Kool-Aid to frazzled dolls, and sold tickets to neighborhood circuses. We never thought twice about cutting across lawns or driveways, though certain houses cloaked with firs and shrubs were reserved as hiding places for the bold in nighttime games of Hide 'n' Seek. To see the inside of a house we would do almost anything: run errands for our parents; sell, door-to-door, Indian corn picked up off the ground of someone's garden; and play with visiting grandchildren. No fences ever blocked our view or entrance. I felt then a freedom and familiarity with my surroundings that I have not felt since.

In the fields stretching directly west and south of our house were the remnants of a failed agricultural venture from my father's childhood days: alfalfa. In the summer my friends and I gathered the scattered purple blossoms and fed them to our pet rabbits. Next to the fields—catty-corner from our backyard—was a series of government-green, two-story apartment buildings. In the late 1920s a country-club-style housing development—Gillespie Gardens—was platted for that area. There were to be circular drives lined with trees, odd-shaped lots, and even a fountain. The streets were to be named Lonegan Lane, Godfrey Avenue, and Georgian Court. But the Depression came along, then the Second World War, and the plans were abandoned. Instead, Gardendale was erected to house the servicemen stationed at the army air force base, east of town. Intended to be torn down after the war, the buildings remained to provide low-income housing and an income for the city.

The population of Gardendale was fairly transient, but some families, especially those with large numbers of children—ten or twelve—became neighborhood institutions. We made up nicknames for several of the children. The most famous was "Glass Bottom." My older sisters were in car pools with many of the Gardendale kids who attended the parochial school across town. By the time I reached school age, however, the Gardendalers were more often the victims of ridicule. In part it was a territorial dispute, but there were undertones of social and racial disparagement.

There were some friendly encounters. A girl on Gillespie played almost exclusively with kids from Gardendale, and a boy from Gardendale was in boy scouts with my brother and other boys in the neighborhood. But usually the liaisons were casual, fostered by proximity rather than similarity, and brief. A little black boy named Omelet (I had never heard of an omelet before and so was annoyed when my mother didn't believe that was his name) came by periodically to visit a balding dog who was tied to a tree bordering on our yard and the Gardendale property. Then for a time there was a family who lived in the apartment building nearest our house. The mother was an American Indian (from "Sou'dacola," one of her youngest children told us), and the father was Mexican-American. When they moved in they had eight girls. The addition of a ninth caused us to dub them the "Ten Little Indians." Hot afternoons we swapped cookies for tortillas with them.

These friendships, however, did not extend beyond the neighborhood, and rarely did we visit one another inside our homes. I was curious about the lives behind those green, stone fronts—I knew they were different from mine; yet when I walked through Gardendale, as a shortcut to someplace else, I hoped no one would think I lived there.

I learned about the streets beyond Gillespie mainly by walking to the library and home from school. I did not know many street names, just those that led to a destination or took me by a special sight. Between First and Second Streets, a block off Walnut, was a yard with a fig tree, a banana tree, and over one hundred varieties of cactus. As soon as the temperatures started dropping in the fall, a greenhouse sprang up magically (so it seemed) to protect this exotic wonder. Fourth Street took my friends and me past Ted's Market, where we could buy candy or popsicles, and on to the zoo. Up one block was Fifth Street and the hospital (QUIET ZONE: we always heeded the sign when we walked by, speaking in hushed tones). Somewhere between there and the library was a castlelike structure with turrets and "SUNNYLAND 1908" imprinted near the top. Sunnyland was divided up into apartments by then, with clotheslines leading out the variously shaped windows and a row of mailboxes lined up on the porch. My parents knew the people who had owned it originally and had been inside several times; my view of it, however, remained that of a wistful admirer.

One day on our way home from the library, on Seventh Street, my neighbor and I decided to remedy our ignorance of street names by looking at all the street signs. Turning east off Seventh onto Walnut, we were delighted to find the names of the streets followed in descending numerical order. We had never suspected such regularity. Not until many years later would I notice the succession of tree streets—Hazel, Hackberry, Walnut, Cedar, Spruce, Pine, Laurel, Chestnut, and Maple—running perpendicular to the number streets, a layout common in towns started by the railroad.

Main Street, one block west of Seventh, I explored most intensely on Saturday afternoons during my last two years of grade school, when my mother finally let me go downtown without her. One of those afternoons a friend and I went into every single store on the street—drugstores, clothing stores, hardware stores, and dime stores. We ended up kneeling in front of a large painting of Christ, in a dark room on the second floor of a furniture store. My mother, no avid shopper herself, marveled that we could spend a whole afternoon downtown without getting bored.

Another afternoon shopping trip, however, ended badly. A friend and I were walking home through Stevens Park, a park square that faces Main Street, when an older boy accosted us by the water fountain. We froze. No weapon was in sight, but his voice was commanding, and his words were threatening. We went up on the bandstand, as he directed, and answered his questions, which at first were innocuous: What did we get for Christmas? How old were we? When he asked us to take off our clothes, however, we found our voices and both screamed no. He took off running and was soon out of sight. My friend and I grabbed hands and ran the ten blocks home, crying all the way. Our mothers called the police, who came and asked us questions. Several weeks later the boy was apprehended. The incident did not stop our trips downtown, but we avoided Stevens Park for several years.

Beyond Main, the streets numbered up to thirteen and then

switched to names of landed Garden Citians. The Holly Sugar Factory, whose name I shared (a coincidence worth a hundred pounds of sugar at my birth), lay beyond. The bulk of the town's Catholics lived in this area, near St. Mary's, the church and school I attended. Despite my many trips there, that section of town was a maze to me—one street coming to a dead end and then starting up again a few blocks later. My mother and I lost our way many times when she took me to birthday parties there.

Garden City pleased me. My parents always followed the same route when driving anywhere, taking the busy streets on the south and north ends of Main—Fulton and Kansas Avenues—and the through streets, Walnut and Fourth. But as a child and a pedestrian, I often took a different way home from school, the library, and the swimming pool, zigzagging to go by favorite landmarks. Each house had its own face, shape, and color, so that, at least east of Main Street, I always knew where I was. There was no danger of mistaking one house for another. Even the enamelled steel prefab Lustron houses of the late 1940s were so few and far between that they, too, had their own identities. Old and new, rich and poor houses sat side by side.

In the mid- to late 1960s, while I was in grade school, the town began spreading far north of Kansas Avenue. The expansion came with a name—"Briar Hill"—that emphasized the singularity in the slight rise in elevation. The first housing development that I was aware of, it featured split-level houses with sliding-glass doors and brick patios and attracted those with steadily increasing incomes. One family on our block, whose children were in their teens, made the move to the "Hill," and the family next door completely remodeled their house in similar fashion. My view of the "Hill" remained that of a bicyclist, panting as I pedaled up Third Street by the tender blades of grass and then whizzing down past the blur of fresh, white paint and brick, my feet on the handlebars. Most of the yards did not have trees, only ornamental shrubs. Landscaping they called it. I envied the people who lived there, except on hot summer days, when they stayed inside with their central air conditioning, while my friends and I in the flatlands remained outside in our shaded yards.

Another expansion affected me more directly when I was in sixth grade. A second Catholic church and grade school were built several blocks east of our house. From Saint Mary's, on Saint John Street, I switched to Saint Dominic's, on J. C. Street ("J. C." did not, as some folks joked, stand for "Jesus Christ"). Saint Mary's had stood as an invincible structure of authority in my mind—both the tall, steepled, dark red brick church and the two-storied, red brick school, topped with a tile roof patronized by cooing pigeons. Saint Dominic's was built of pale yellow brick and had only one story and no trees. The school, which was connected to the church (or "multipurpose room" as it was called—it doubled as a cafeteria) was modern and lenient, without precedent. It was air conditioned, and each classroom had a sink. The six-graders played a new game—tetherball—and had three recesses, along with the first-graders.

Other enterprises followed Saint Dominic's in the move eastward. The junior college moved out beyond the church, and soon brick houses and duplexes filled street after street. My family no longer lived on the edge of town.

Sometime during my adolescence, Garden City began to seem less pleasing. Sunday afternoons, when I was in junior high school, my friends and I took long walks in search of excitement. Peripatetics, we walked aimlessly down the middle of residential streets, cut across freshly mowed lawns, and peered through the gaps in picket fences. Despite its growth, the town was beginning to seem small.

In high school the walks turned to drives, the paved residential streets to dirt country roads. They never led anywhere, but at least they gave me the illusion of getting away. The dust kicked up by the tires confirmed my growing suspicion that the life I wanted lay elsewhere.

During this time, the late 1960s and early 1970s, the texture of life in Garden City also began to change. Food franchises came to town, formula recipes for chicken and pizza standardizing our taste buds, burgers still belonging to the realm of drive-ins. Grocery stores went discount, and the city commission voted to intall piped-in music downtown to give it that "shopping center atmosphere." Local DJs imitated the Top-40, big-city sound, determining our taste in music.

Seeing them vaguely as signs of progress, I welcomed most of these changes. I did not connect them with the dissatisfaction I felt with my life in Garden City, the smallness I sensed around me that was not so much a matter of size as of attitude, expectation, ambition. Given some distance, though, I could have come up with a similar diagnosis for the two of us: both the town and I were pushed simultaneously toward conformity—it because of prosperity, I because of my age and sex. The attitude of the town changed from one of upkeep to one of keeping up. Similarly, I felt compelled to compete with people I barely knew for things I barely wanted. Life, like the catsup in the drive-ins, seemed thin and watered down.

Toward the end of my senior year in high school the old alfalfa field next to our house was divided up into lots and sold. Soon after, a white open-porched house belonging to the hospital nuns was moved from Fourth Street to the end of the block, the hospital having expanded. The nuns no sooner moved in than grass was growing, and trees were planted to replace those uprooted. But looking out the window of our kitchen door, I noticed that the house blocked our view of Evans Street.

During my first few years away from home, I sometimes fantasized that Garden City would become a ghost town, like my mother's hometown, in northwest Kansas. We passed the town on the way to visit my grandmother, in Nebraska. Sometimes we turned off the highway and drove down the dirt streets, looking for houses my mother once knew. Then we drove down the wide Main Street, past the boarded-up general store and the charred, car-motors building. To my siblings and me the hollow shells were curiosities; but for my mother they were like people she had once known.

Behind my idle wish for Garden City's demise, perhaps, was a desire to outlive the town, to fix it firmly in my past. I knew I would not live in Garden City again, and yet when I was away from it I felt its presence in my automatic comparisons with other places I lived, other people I met. If the town ceased to exist physically—except for a few crumbling buildings and a grain elevator—I would be free to select whatever memories I wanted from it and not have to watch it turn into some other place.

A few fires—the American Legion building and a grade school (set afire by students)—may have lit my hopes of an apocalypse temporarily, but the damage was quickly repaired, the charred remains not allowed to blow in the wind. Garden City would not take the course of gradual deterioration like other smaller towns around it. Across the country, gas prices rose and the speed limit fell; on my college campus the light switches in dormitory hallways were taped down to conserve energy; and E. F. Schumacher's *Small Is Beautiful* was making classroom syllabi. But in Garden City in the mid-1970s, largely because of the business precipitated by pivot irrigation, they were talking boom.

In terms of population, boom was a bit of an exaggeration. Garden City gained a thousand or so every two years. The 1960 census listed it at 11,000; in 1974, when I left home, it had reached 18,000. There were more telling signs of growth: the number of water towers from my childhood increased from one to four; and total employment for Finney County more than doubled, from around 5,500 in 1960 to 12,000 in 1977.

The changes in the neighborhoods since I left home have been dramatic. With the rapid multiplication of housing developments, income has become a major factor in determining where residents live in Garden City. On top of Briar Hill extends a middle- to upper-middle-class development, Labrador Ridge, the streets of which are supposedly named for labrador dogs the developer has known (including one named "Easy"). Further east the slope has been dubbed Indian Hill, a development that features houses and yards smaller and more uniform than those on Labrador Ridge. (When the city limits were extended to include these houses, many of the dirt roads used for parking during my high-school days were paved over.) Those with wide-open budgets for wide-open spaces live southwest of the city limits, in Sagebrush Estates (in the sandhills), or southeast of the city, near the new Southwind Country Club.

Low-income modular housing is available in the northwest section of town, downhill and downwind from one of the major feedyards. Golf Acres, a free-for-all housing development, east of town by the old Country Club, offers five-acre tracts to do with what you will. A brief tour of Golf Acres that I took in the early 1980s revealed an assortment of trailers, makeshift used-car lots, cardboard rental housing, and a southern-style pillared mansion with a gaggle of Canada geese in front. Out on Highway 50, beyond the airport, I saw a sign proclaiming "Rolling Hills Estates." It consisted of a couple of trailers and some water wells next to a prairie-dog village. No hills had rolled in yet. At the east edge of town, near the new overpass, a sign has been posted in a field: "Cloverleaf Junction Subdivision."

Keeping track of and guessing the names of the new developments has become something of a sport, but the developments themselves have considerably altered the arrangement of the town. Garden City has suburbs. The newer grade schools have been built in the northeast section of town (along the multinamed hill) and accommodate, almost exclusively, white, middle- or upper-middle-class students, while the older schools in the west part of town have more minorities and low-income families. When an additional junior high school was built in the far northeast section, the school board had to draw the dividing lines to ensure that the legal racial balance at the two schools could be maintained, which meant that some students, mostly the Chicanos who lived south of the tracks, attended the school farther from their homes. Bussing in Garden City is no longer just for farm kids.

Property values have come to be vigorously defended, not because superhighways threaten to disturb the quiet of residential areas, but because the potential use of vacant lots threatens to disturb the socioeconomic equanimity of some neighborhoods. Several years ago it took two attempts to get the city commission to approve a request to rezone an area east of town for the housing of several hundred Southeast Asians brought in by Iowa Beef Processors. And on Gillespie: when a back lot was donated to a preschool for mentally and physically handicapped children, some of the neighbors filed suit.

As for the rest of Gillespie—three houses have been built in the field next to my parents' house, making the score of the north side to the south side eight and seven (where formerly it was eight and three). The uprooting of the trees has made that end of the block much sunnier; it is no longer used for an in-town lovers' lane. Tall, wooden fences were erected to block the view of Gardendale from the backyards. Divorces and deaths have caused the occupancy of the older houses on the block to shift so often that a few houses remain vacant most of the time. The house on the northwest corner seems to be painted a new color every time I visit.

Those were the kinds of changes I noticed first: new neighborhoods devoid of imagination or memories, the condemning and subsequent closing of all the downtown hotels, and the multiplication of burger franchises and bank branches east of town. Garden City was undergoing a small-time imitation of urban sprawl.

But there have also been unexpected wellsprings of life. The zoo, which had begun to deteriorate before I left home, now has an organized group of supporters, who have raised money and volunteered labor to improve the conditions for the animals. The lions and tigers, for instance, now roam in large, fenced tracts of land instead of pacing in dingy, smelly cages. The Big Pool, threatened with destruction, was instead renovated. Downtown, as of 1982, had managed to hold its own, a proposed shopping center still nothing but a sign along the highway.

In some respects Garden City has not changed all that much from my days there. I can still walk (alone, at night) through the central part of town—the railroad grid—and easily recall moments from my childhood. Other places I have lived have grown at a more phenomenal rate, on a much larger scale. In Garden City change is humanly fathomable. Comparison is still possible. I know what was before. I know what has taken its place. And there are pauses in between.

Home for Christmas one year after college, I discovered the city had finally gone through with its promise of forty years before: Gardendale had been torn down. Only the trees and playground equipment and one pale yellow building, which housed the public mental health clinic, remained. It felt empty. No clotheslines sagging with jeans and shirts and dresses, no mothers screeching at their kids in high-pitched voices, and no kids for my youngest sister to share tortillas with.

In 1982 when I was visiting, the north edge of the field had been zoned for a condominium development—multiple family dwellings, but requiring a higher income bracket—and a new public mental health building was under construction in the southeast corner. But the rest of the field stretched out in splendid spaciousness. Grackles congregated in the trees, and parents brought their children to play on the remaining swings. Plans for the space were still uncertain; a new library, a park, and more public service buildings had all been suggested. But for awhile it was still a vacant lot, an open field, a case of arrested development. And through the back-door window of my parents' kitchen, I could once more see through to Evans.

Illustrations

ARKANSAS RIVER—WET. In July, 1878, the year settlers started coming to Garden City, the Arkansas River stretched from one end of the bridge to the other. (Courtesy of the Kansas State Historical Society)

ARKANSAS RIVER—DRY. During the fall and winter of 1903–1904, the view from the bridge was a dry riverbed. (Courtesy of the Kansas State Historical Society)

THE BIG POOL—1954. Since it opened in 1922, the Big Pool has been the most reliable body of water in Garden City. (Courtesy of the Finney County Historical Society)

WESTERN KANSAS LANDSCAPE I. Patches of native beauty appear in the uncultivated parts of western Kansas. (Courtesy of Quentin Hope)

WESTERN KANSAS LANDSCAPE II. Outside towns, trees seldom impede the view of the horizon. (Courtesy of Quentin Hope)

PART TWO

Bright, talented people who grow up in rural areas typically leave home at an early age, returning only for visits. Throughout the 1970s and early 1980s, in Garden City, however, that pattern was altered. While many young people did leave, others, having worked and gone to college elsewhere, returned—with their own plans for Garden City. Their homecoming sparked a sort of cultural renaissance in the area as these individuals brought fresh ideas, experiences, and skills to local politics, the arts, education, the media, and the legal system.

In the summer and fall of 1982 I interviewed several of these individuals about where they had been, what they had done, and why they had returned.

Two days behind the dust-storm—man's
Fecklessness, God's wrath—and once
Dust on the highway piled so deep
Mules had to drag the car. This

Was Kansas, and in midafternoon
It rained blood for half an hour—
Or what looked red as blood, and what
Bible or folklore would call a rain

of blood. It never rained any frogs,
Just blood. Then Garden City. What
a hell of a name! Dust heaped aside,
Faces stunned white. Eyes blank like those

Of people picked up in a lifeboat, the only
Survivors. "Whar goen?" This getting gas.
"Californ-ya, hanh? Not me. Out thar
Some day they'll git somethin wuss. I'll jist

Stick whar I knows whut the wust is." [1]

—FROM ROBERT PENN WARREN'S
"TRIPS TO CALIFORNIA"

Our consciousness, by which we live, is itself but the creature of
variety. Upon what food does it subsist in such a land? What liveli-
hood can repay a human creature for a life spent in this huge
sameness?

—ROBERT LOUIS STEVENSON UPON CROSSING
THE HIGH PLAINS IN 1892

[1] From *Being Here: Poetry 1977–1980* by Robert Penn Warren. Copyright ©
1978, 1979, 1980 by Robert Penn Warren. Reprinted by permission of Random
House, Inc.

CHAPTER 6

His Eminence

ABOUT 12:30 ON A JULY AFTERNOON, my phone rang.

"Where are you?"

"It's only twelve—oh, you eat dinner at noon, don't you?"

"City folks. Well, come out for supper then."

Earlier that week I had run into the caller, Jay Brown, at a forum of 1982 Kansas Republican gubernatorial candidates. While they were voicing unanimous support for capital punishment, Jay, a long-time Democrat, practiced a question for them: "I know these things are difficult to predict, but could you give a ball-park estimate of how many people you expect to execute your first year in office?"

The irreverence of this tall, twenty-seven-year-old farmer with straight brown hair, a freckled face, and big feet was familiar to me. In high school we were novice debate partners for a year and acted in several plays together. At the end of the year he wrote in my yearbook, "You know, I thought I didn't like you at the beginning of the year, but after debate and drama I'm sure of it."

Having missed dinner but hoping to arrive in time for supper, I set out early for the thirty-mile drive from Garden City to Eminence Route. Taking Highway 156 east, past the nineteen-mile marker, I turned left onto a dirt road, where the Charleston grain-elevator sign used to be (according to Jay's instructions). I followed the ruts in the center of the road over the occasional hills and made a right at the first opportunity.

Around a bend and off to the right an old stone house and a barn appeared.

Home to three generations of Browns, the small house originally served as the post office for the town of Eminence, in what was then Garfield County. Like many small towns in Kansas around the turn of the century, Eminence was the victim of a county-seat battle. The remains of its arch rival, Ravanna, can still be seen several miles away. Ravanna held the title first, by virtue of a vote of 467 to 432 in its favor. When it was determined, though, that the ballot box had been stuffed—a matter of forty-six votes—the title reverted to Eminence. A few years later Ravanna had the county resurveyed and discovered that it was just short of the 432 square miles required by state law. In 1893 the land was annexed to Finney County, making it the second largest county (in area) in the state and causing the demise of both towns. Unlike many other battles for the county seat, no lives were lost, except for that of a horse that happened in the way of an errant bullet.

I continued up the road a mile or so to a newer house, where Jay's parents, a dog, and numerous cats lived. Since Jay had become the sole occupant of the former post office, the food supply there had dwindled. Once when Mr. and Mrs. Brown left him, his older brother Jerry, and a hired hand to fend for themselves for a week, Jay immediately volunteered to do all the dishes. The other two agreed for a couple of days and then decided that it was Jay's turn to cook. When they came in from the field later that day, they found that Jay had set the table properly and had placed a Snickers bar on each plate.

Not who was going to cook but what was being cooked was the issue when I arrived at the Browns'. Mrs. Brown had received some garden vegetables from a friend and had tried out a recipe for stuffed spaghetti squash. "I don't know how it will taste. Try it, and if you don't like it, you can have some meat and potatoes." Tall and lean like Jay, Mrs. Brown did not remind me of the short, plump farmwives who hovered over the food and sewing exhibits at the county fair. Her voice was gravelly, matter-of-fact. She had a smoker's cough.

Mr. Brown sat at one end of the table. His hair stood up short and stiff, like the bristles of a scrub brush. His skin was sun darkened and tough, like an orange peel. I could not see his eyes, which were squinting at the squash. He and Jay poked at the stuffing with their forks and asked where the spaghetti was. After one helping each they dug into the roast beef and mashed potatoes. The meal at noon was much better, they all agreed.

After supper Jay and I headed out to the garage, stepping carefully among the kittens on the floor. We ignored Mrs. Brown's offer of free kittens.

Passing Jay's pickup, I noticed a shotgun on the seat.

"Prairie dogs."

We decided to take my car.

Before turning out of the driveway onto the road, I pressed my foot lightly on the brakes.

"Generally out here you don't have to stop and look both directions." Jay looked at me levelly and spoke in a monotone.

I turned right and headed back toward Jay's house. Nothing but fields separated the two Brown houses, but earlier in Jay's life more houses, more Browns, and more traffic existed along Eminence Route. In 1939, Jay's paternal grandparents moved into the house in which he now lived. Later one of their sons and his wife moved across the road and lived with their five children in a house since blown down by a tornado. Jay's parents, along with his brother and himself, lived farther down the road in a one-room house, also no longer standing.

Jay talked fondly about living there. During the summer they kept watermelons outside in a big tank of water. "That's how we lost my younger brother," he once told me. "Bobbing for watermelons."

I reminded him of the story.

"Naw. It was really just to keep the watermelons cool."

In 1959, Jay's uncle, who had always had a bad heart, was put in the hospital. It was about the same time that the Clutters, who lived in Holcomb, on the other side of Garden City, but who farmed land around the Browns, were murdered.

"Everybody was scared being out by themselves at night," Jay said. "Locking doors, getting their guns." In the early 1960s, after his uncle died, everybody else moved to town, and Jay and his family moved into his grandfather's house.

As we drove toward this house, we passed a field of alfalfa in bloom, and a sweet scent drifted through the open window. I told Jay about a short story in which a farmer, in celebration of the death of his domineering wife, plants all his fields to sweet peas—just to see the flowers and smell the perfume. He laughed. For about fifteen years the Browns had a thousand acres planted to alfalfa. "That was really something," said Jay. He looked across the purple blur outside the window. A perennial crop, alfalfa is planted only once and can be harvested several times a year. These plants were old, though, and the Browns, like most of their neighbors, put their efforts and acres into cash crops, wheat and milo.

Jay saw little romance in American agriculture, calling it "primarily a business with a lot of science in it." He mentioned a recent article in a farm magazine that predicted that by the year 2000 every farmer would have to own a home computer. The folklore of his grandfather's day had been plowed under. "Lots of planting superstitions. Plant by the moon if it's a full moon. All that rot. We've gotten away from that pretty much."

Scientists and county extension agents, however, did not rank high in Jay's estimation either. "It's all real good when you're working up there on a little patch. But when you come out and plant a thousand acres of wheat, that's a lot different. If you've got your whole future riding on it, you're going to use something tried and true."

Jay was reminded of an incident from John Kenneth Galbraith's account of his experiences as ambassador to India. Farmers from Kansas and Oklahoma had traveled to India to show the farmers how to plant their crops. "The Indian farmers, realizing that if they didn't get a crop they were going to starve to death, generally stayed with the traditional means, much to the annoyance of the experts." All in all, Jay figured, the true expert on growing food was the farmer with experience. "Wheat farmers, we always think we're the bastion of common sense."

That skepticism toward science is an attitude engendered, perhaps, by the uncontrollable elements with which farmers must contend. Advances in herbicides, hybrids, and tillage techniques mean little to them in the face of droughts, hailstorms, or tornadoes. "Like last year we had a beautiful wheat crop, and then it froze May 15 and pfffft. We went out there, and it was all gone. Two years ago we had a lot of hail damage. People who aren't farmers don't have any conception, I think, of how important the weather is to us. If you're getting a paycheck, working at a normal job, the weather doesn't make any difference to you. But when it can make or break your crop or even your whole farm, then it's a lot more important to you."

"What about this obsession with weather forecasts that farmers have? If you're going to get hailed out, you're going to get hailed out. What difference does it make if you know about it thirty minutes in advance?"

"People like to know what's going to happen." Jay grew animated. "They like to have reports four times an hour. And updates. And severe-storm warnings with little beeps on the radio so they know something terrible is going to happen. Of course, some get a little carried away." Jay chuckled. "There's one farmer over here who can kill the crop twenty times before it's harvested: 'Boy, it's got mosaic in it,' or 'Boy, it's got greenbug in it,' or 'Boy, it's going to hail.' Some farmers are just doomsayers."

So far in 1982 the weather had been good to western Kansas. Bountiful rains in June delayed harvest of the winter wheat a bit but brought welcome moisture to the corn and milo, as well as all the incidental vegetation crowding the ditches alongside the road. The creek that we passed over, in which Jay had fished as a boy and an uncle had drowned in the 1950s, had water in it for the first time in years. In the calm of the evening, verdant fields stretching to the horizon, growing seemed effortless in this country.

Jay knew better. The low average rainfall means farmers

in western Kansas must take special precautions with the land. "We have to make sure that the ground is covered at all times with some sort of vegetation so that the topsoil doesn't blow away and use as few processes on the land as possible to conserve moisture. And we have to summer fallow, whereas farmers in eastern Kansas can have continuous crops: plow one up and plant another." Farming in western Kansas is an unnatural act.

Despite the numerous advances made in irrigation, Jay's family and most of their neighbors in northeastern Finney County continued as dryland farmers. No giant walking sprinklers or pipes appeared in the fields surrounding Jay and me.

"Why don't you irrigate?"

"Just the expense. The costs of the equipment and the gas or the electricity to run it were too prohibitive for us to ever consider it. To be able to start irrigating in the early 1970s, you almost had to own and have paid for your land."

Of the four thousand-plus acres that they oversaw in 1982, Jay's parents owned only 160 acres (the size of a homestead), and his brother Jerry and his wife owned another 160. The rest they rented from various landlords living in Garden City, Florida, and the Northeast. The Browns used only half the land for growing crops, and half of that laid fallow. The other two thousand acres or so, unsuitable for farming, they used as pasture for cattle.

"A lot of the land around here is fairly marginal, real sandy. It really wouldn't have adapted itself well to irrigation."

Geological maps of the area, in fact, show that the Ogallala Aquifer does not extend far into the northeast part of Finney County. Underlying most of the area is Carlisle shale, which provides little or no water, and the Niobrara formation, with massive beds of chalk and limestone, which supply only a limited amount of water.

A certain provincialism, Jay added, also would prevent some of his neighbors from ever irrigating. "A lot of people out here are set. They don't irrigate and won't irrigate ever. They've been dryland farmers all their lives and so just won't do it."

Jay had had a brief experience with irrigation on a small scale one summer, when his family rented twenty-seven acres of milo that was irrigated by pipe. "That was more of a problem than anything: open up the gates, check them every morning and every evening. It was just such a bother—for what we ever got out of it." Jay was relieved that none of their landlords ever asked them to irrigate.

Other farmers, Jay said, had not been as fortunate. A neighboring family refused to irrigate when their landlord asked them to because they could not afford it. The landlord said he would find someone else who would do it, and the family, who had farmed for thirty years, was forced out.

"Is there a lot of friction between dryland farmers and irrigators?"

"Not a lot. Some things—like when you see someone irrigating after or while it's raining, or letting the water run off into the ditches, that's pretty irritating. A few years back a neighbor over here who is surrounded by irrigators found the well for their house had gone dry. They had to drill another a mile away. That causes a lot of hard feelings."

"Do you think the Ogallala will dry up in forty years?"

"I think it will be a lot lower than it is." Jay paused. "I think the state's going to have to start regulating it a lot more, putting limits on what people can pump. Some people have been talking about these goofy schemes of bringing water all the way from Canada, the Missouri River. That's crazy. That's just wishful thinking. I think most people out here will be broke before that ever happens."

According to Jay rising energy costs may be the best hope for the survival of the Ogallala. Along with the use and fuel-adjustment charges that irrigators pay for power, they must also pay a surcharge on their peak demand—the greatest amount of power used in any fifteen-minute period in a month. "It's getting so expensive for these guys to irrigate that a lot of them are having to cut back, which I think is a good thing."

A water depletion allowance, Jay added, enabled irrigators to collect on their losses, however, providing an incentive to use up the water while they could, at the expense of other farmers in the area, not to mention future generations of farmers.

"I think farmers try to stab each other in the back." Jay chuckled. "Mencken had a story about some farmers—'gaping primates' he called them—who were going to swindle the government. They got together and decided they wouldn't plant very much wheat, drive the prices way up, and really put the screws to the consumers. Then all the farmers ran out and planted all the wheat they could to take advantage of what they figured the other guy wasn't going to plant. So there was a tremendous surplus. Then they went crying to the government to help bail them out."

That ambivalent attitude toward the role that the government should play in agriculture still persisted. "Farmers are pretty hypocritical. Like now they complain that the state department is botching up everything with the grain embargoes, keeping the prices down. They never want the government to interfere. But when hard times come, then they want the government to come in and help them out with disaster payments or loans. I think most people are like that, though: if things are going well, you don't want to be bothered; but if things are going bad, then you want help."

Irrigation only exacerbated the circularity of farmers' problems. By doubling the number of bushels per acre, it almost assured a yearly surplus of certain crops in the United States. Because they were paying at least twice as much for power and fertilizer as the dryland farmer, irrigators had to produce or overproduce just to break even. But surpluses are more a bane than a boon to farmers. Bumper crops may represent a victory over the caprices of nature, but before they can reap any profit, farmers must deal with another, more formidable, adversary: the market.

"Ten years ago it was great out here. Prices were going up. We had pretty good crops—not great crops. Interest rates were low, so you could borrow money every year. All your expenses were lower. Things have changed a lot in ten years."

The price of land also went up in those years, enabling farmers to borrow against it. Some overextended themselves.

Later, when production costs skyrocketed and land was deval-ued, a lot of those farmers were in trouble.

Even farmers who did not overextend themselves, including the Browns, were seeing hard times. In 1980 another Brown family moved off Eminence Route. Jay's brother Jerry (who started farming with his father in the early 1970s after gradu-ating from college) and his wife and son were forced to leave the farm when they could not get a loan. The price of machin-ery, energy, and fertilizer had doubled, tripled, and qua-drupled, while the price of wheat had remained almost the same as it had been twenty years earlier. Four thousand acres, it was decided, were not enough to support two families (five people). Jerry and his family left the house Jay's parents now live in and moved to Denver, where Jerry became a commodi-ties broker.

"That was a bad thing. I never expected this family would ever have to break up like that. That was too bad." Jay cleared his throat. "I was hoping when I decided to come back that they would all be here, but they couldn't. I can work out here because I'm not a partner. I can work just as a laborer, and Mom and Dad can take if off their taxes. That way it's a lot easier for them."

Even with just the three of them, the Browns were having a difficult time staying in farming. In 1981, when the freak frost in May killed their wheat crop, Jay's parents joked about how they would have to take up robbing banks to hold onto their farm. "Anymore, if you have just one bad year, you can be out. Most of it's just interest rates, the price of fuel. No room for error anymore. If you ever come way in debt—like if you have to buy new machinery—and you lose something, you're finished."

To help out, Mrs. Brown, who refused to drive grain trucks during harvest, took an interest in marketing. She listened daily to the market reports on the radio and kept in close con-tact with a commodities broker.

Unlike other farmers in 1979, the Browns did not drive their tractors to Washington. "That was silly—plowing up, striking, not producing. We couldn't afford to. We had to pro-

duce." Jay paused and grinned slowly. "Blowing up silos—
that would be better. A little more militant action. The farmers
have the wrong idea. They should start attacking the grain
companies. Those are the people making money. They make
money whether the price of grain goes up or down. Those are
the ones you want to get." He narrowed his eyes to slits. "Start
lynching commodities brokers. Lynch a few hundred, and the
rest will learn their lesson."

"What about your brother?"

Jay shrugged. "I told him—one of these days I'm going to
have to hang him."

Part of our conversation took place in front of Jay's house,
near a grapevine that, perpetually watered by a leaky pump
handle, crept up an old windmill. Farm vehicles in various
states of dismemberment lay about. Jay shook his head.
"Things are always breaking down."

"Do you ever wish you farmed in Iowa?"

"Naw. Too humid. Too much rain. Corn. A lot of people
don't think there's much in Kansas, but I think it's pretty. I like
the grass and pastures and wheat—it's just nice seeing the
wheat grow. This area right in here is nice because we're down
in a little valley with a little crick. We have more trees. There
are parts of western Kansas I wouldn't care to live in. Just flat
like a board. No trees. Nothing out there."

Yellow cats of all sizes stalked the grounds. One named
Johnson (Samuel) rubbed against my leg. Jay stooped to pick
up a kitten, and we went into the house.

On the kitchen wall, above a clock stuck at 4:45, hung a
woodcut of a mild-looking John Brown.

"Any relation?"

Jay did not hear me. His head was lodged in the refrigerator,
which was empty except for beer and a few vegetables from
his mother's garden. He emerged with two beers and we
moved to his living room. He fingered through his record collection and selected Chopin—"the George Jones of his day."
Settling back on the couch underneath a picture of a locomo-
tive, Jay sighed. "I always liked living in the country—except
for having to go to work when I got home from school."

He attended Theoni, a country school with eight grades, sixty pupils. "All farm kids. There were five in my class."

"Were you first in your class?"

"I was the biggest. Does that count for anything?"

In ninth grade Jay took the bus into Garden City. "I hated the junior high. That was a bad time. We had all been out here eight years. I didn't know anybody in town. Dang city kids."

Things improved in high school, when he became involved in debate and drama and made some friends. Unlike Jerry, he did not participate in FFA—Future Farmers of America—or any other agricultural activities. "When I was in high school I didn't have any intention of ever becoming a farmer. I always wanted to do something else, go off someplace."

The year after he graduated from high school he traveled in the eastern and southern United States and farmed. The next year he went off to college.

He chose Antioch College, a small, private, liberal-arts school of about one thousand, situated in Yellow Springs, Ohio. He was attracted by its work-study program, which alternated periods of academic work on campus with periods of work experience off campus, known as co-ops. For one co-op Jay spent a summer in Boston working for the Sierra Club; during the others he worked on the farm.

"Antioch was all right, but a little hectic." The constant strikes and perpetual financial upheaval of the college wore on Jay after awhile. And he found some of the political attitudes went against his grain. "It was fashionable to be radical, so everyone was radical. It didn't make any difference if it had any sense behind it or not." After two years there he returned to Kansas and farmed for another three years. "After you've been someplace else, it's nice to come back and be a farmer."

He returned to school mainly at the prompting of his parents, neither of whom had gone to college. "That's sort of a family deal. You don't do that so much for yourself. All my grandparents were happy. Some family pride there—grandkids going to college. They didn't really care what you did with it. Just nice to know you went."

Jay claimed that he selected McGill University, in Montreal, because it was situated in a big city that had a baseball team. When I visited him there in the spring of 1980, he was collecting newspaper clippings about the precarious state of Tito's health and taping them on the door of his dormitory room. He graduated the following spring, with a degree in political science.

Gradually he had given up any thoughts of going to graduate school or law school. "Too tedious. I got bored with college. I was ready to quit. It wasn't hard. It just didn't seem like it was worth it." He paused. "I always thought college would be great if there weren't so many students around. At McGill you could never look out your window without seeing people. I like Kansas, where nobody's going to bother you."

Without those years away from Kansas, though, Jay would have been desperate to go anywhere. "I may even have become a county extension agent and moved to South Dakota."

Jay's years away at college could be viewed as a sort of cultural exchange. "Most Easterners, most city people don't have any idea what it's like to farm, don't have any idea about the expense or the time or what we do. So it's always a revelation to them to know anything about farming." At Antioch he found that most people had an idyllic view. "If you asked anyone if they'd rather live in the country or the city, ninety-nine out of a hundred would say, 'Oh, live in the country. Work on a farm. Be your own boss. Do whatever you want.' I tried to explode as many of those myths as I could."

In Boston people were more interested in his accent. "When they heard you talk, they'd always ask if you were from Alabama or Mississippi—some nether region of the country." At McGill people were more snobbish. One student asked him, "What in Gawd's name would you do on a farm in Kawnsas?"

A few of Jay's friends from around the country had ventured out to Eminence Route to find out. The most memorable visit was from a friend that he had met at Antioch. Covering the 1976 Republican National Convention, in Kansas City, for ABC, he decided to drive out to see Jay. Jay laughed. "He just hated it out here. Hated not having anybody around, not being able to see buildings, not being able to go to town in five min-

utes. He told me I had to get out of here, had to get back to
school." Even more amusing, though, was his account of the
harrowing trip back across the state. "I think he'd seen *Easy
Rider* four or five times, so he was sure some farmers were
going to take him out and beat him up when they found out he
was from New Jersey. He wrote me about being pulled over
for speeding in Great Bend, farmers with their gun racks in
their pickups cruising by—he knew he'd never get out of town
alive. He was a fairly neurotic fellow."

Other friends declined Jay's invitations. One in Philadelphia
said that she could never stand the quiet. His roommate in
Boston backed out when Jay told him that there were more
people living in Boston than in the whole state of Kansas.

The solitude that unnerved his urban friends was exactly
what appealed to Jay about living on the farm. "I always liked
being by myself, not having anybody around. It's nice every
once in awhile just to be off by yourself—except for cats." He
threw a pen at the yellow kitten playing with a lamp cord. He
claimed that he made the trip to town once, maybe twice a
month to check out the bookstore, to buy groceries, or to see
a movie. "I'm a homebody. I figure if people want to, they
can come out and see me."

Even then, visitors faced stiff competition. The walls surrounding us were lined with floor-to-ceiling bookshelves filled
with the complete works of Joseph Conrad, in twenty-six volumes; Jane Austen, in seven volumes; fourteen volumes of
Dickens; Volumes I and II of Carlyle's *French Revolution;* the
compact edition of the *Oxford English Dictionary;* the *Encyclopedia of Philosophy;* the *New Columbia Encyclopedia;* and
the *Baseball Encyclopedia.* Upstairs, past the American and
Confederate flags hanging on either wall, was his Civil War
library, which contained 120 volumes of the *War of the Re-
bellion: Official Records of the Union and Confederate Ar-
mies.* Literature filled the other shelves.

I recalled a party at this house several years before. Jay disappeared periodically while everyone else was playing cha-
rades in the kitchen. Concerned, I went in search of him and
found him off in a room by himself, reading a magazine.

"A lot of people wonder what on earth you could do with so many books. Most farmers, they read farm magazines. Maybe newspapers."

The Browns had always been readers. Slow winter months and an occasional rainy day provided them with plenty of reading time. The diary of Samuel Pepys, who was always "vexed" by his wife, was currently amusing Jay. The previous winter's project was Proust's *Remembrance of Things Past.* Sometimes he reread his grandfather's classics, which he first read as a child. "That's one thing I like about being out of college: now I have time to reread all those books I had to rush through."

To keep up with current affairs Jay had a daily subscription to the *New York Times* (which usually arrived just two days late—only a day later than the *Garden City Telegram*) and subscriptions to *Atlantic Monthly, Harper's, Wilson Quarterly, American Scholar, Newsweek, Time, New Republic,* and the *New York Review of Books.* He belonged to several book clubs as well. And "when things got to bearing down after awhile," he made a trip to Denver or some farther outpost.

As a child Jay had dreamed of writing history books. He had one in mind as we talked—a biography of Boston Corbett, the man who shot John Wilkes Booth. "A real strange character." Jay rubbed his hands together. "He was a religious fanatic. He castrated himself after being approached by two prostitutes. Later, after he shot Booth, he went on to become sergeant at arms in the Kansas House of Representatives, and one day he went loony and started taking shots at all the legislators. They put him away, but he escaped. Nobody ever heard of him again. I'd like to find out if there are any diaries or letters. I think he's real interesting—one of the great screwballs in American history."

The hour grew late, and I left His Eminence to put out the cat and dispose of the beer cans. Pulling out of the driveway, barely hesitating at the intersection, I headed out in the dark toward the highway. A large, dark shape loomed ahead on the road. I slowed down, and a cow lumbered off to the side. A few minutes later a star fell from the sky, its tail streaming behind.

CHAPTER 7

Where You're At

"A LOT OF THINGS I WANT TO DO on stage are impossible. Like I want people to jump up and freeze in the air. Or jump up and run in place, like in the old cartoons. And my students try so hard for me, but so far no one's been able to get more than one-and-a-half revolutions with their feet before they hit the floor." She laughed and pulled a cigarette to her lips. The smoke curling out of her mouth reminded me of the caterpillar's hookah in *Alice in Wonderland,* and I got the feeling that contradictions rarely bothered her.

I first saw Skip in the summer of 1982 during a dress rehearsal of a community-theater production of *Cabaret.* Dressed in layers—tights, leotard, Atlanta Ballet sweatshirt, leg warmers, and jazz shoes—she paced up and down the stage, directing with a cigarette. A blue bandanna was tied underneath a thick, reddish-brown braid, which hung down the middle of her back. Her hands and face followed every movement and word of the actors. A few days later I talked with her in her office, just above the community-college auditorium.

I asked her about her name "Skip." "My father gave that to me before I was born. It didn't matter if I was a boy or a girl." Legally her name was Doral—a name her grandmother had heard back in Kentucky. When she was growing up in southwest Kansas, though, no one else had heard it until the hotel in Florida was built and the cigarette came out, so she stuck with "Skip." "People get really tense, you know, when you give them a name that they're not familiar with."

Her married name—Mancini—caused her even more problems in 1972, when she returned to southwest Kansas, where she taught dance and theater for the community college and the city recreation commission, in Garden City. "I guess because it's Italian or because it's not what all the other names here are, people get really freaked out." A woman at a dry-cleaning establishment came to mind. "I've been going there for years, and she still can't spell my last name. She knows my name, and she knows how to pronounce it, but she can't figure out how to spell it. She starts crossing it out. She gets really involved—sometimes my dry-cleaning ticket has eight or ten cross outs." Skip laughed. "Finally I said, 'Let's go on a first-name basis. We really know each other very well.'"

Skip was used to not quite fitting in. For the first four years of her life her father was off serving in World War II. When he returned they moved around Oklahoma while her father worked as a roughneck on oil rigs. Then he enrolled at the University of Oklahoma, completing a five-year pharmacy program in three years while working at a drugstore nights and roughnecking on weekends to support Skip and her mother. When Skip was eight or nine they moved to Sublette, Kansas, thirty-five miles south of Garden City. Her father still ran a drugstore there.

"It was a very tight community. I think that's still the case here—I mean with anyone moving into the area. A lot of people would argue and they'd say, 'No, no, it's so friendly.' Well, it's friendly if you have the same background. And it's friendly if you aren't different. But I was very different because of where I came from—the oil-field life and that whole thing. Also I worked—at my father's drugstore. And that was different. In Sublette in the fifties there was a division between the working class and the farming class. Helping out with harvest was one thing. But if you worked at a cafe or a store, it took a little while to be accepted."

Skip spent her childhood swimming, listening to 45-rpm classical records on the little record player her father bought her, and reading every book (except the deeds and abstracts, she qualified) in the Haskell County Library. In high school she had an English teacher who encouraged her interest in literature and the humanities. But the school offered no foreign languages, no theater, nothing extracurricular, except band. She tried that for awhile, but found that it was not what she had in mind. "I don't want it to sound like I sat off by myself and read books all the time, because that wasn't the case. It was just that most of the activities that were available through the school or through churches were tremendously conforming."

After high school Skip attended OU, her father's alma mater. Her first two years there she double majored in pre-med, to please her father, and theater, to please herself. When the combination became too much to handle, she gave up her father's dream and pursued her own. "I was never going to amount to anything as far as he was concerned." She laughed. "We're on very good terms now, but at times I think he still lays awake at night thinking about that, grumbling in the back of his mind for my disappointing him."

In 1964, after graduating, Skip left for San Francisco State College. It was different. A street-car school. "You went out there, and you went to your classes and signed your petitions for that day, and you fought through the lines of whoever was picketing what, and then you got on the streetcar and went back to Berkeley or wherever."

She spent two years there earning a Master's in professional theater and becoming the first student ever to have a production thesis accepted. Her show was Tennessee Williams's *Orpheus Descending,* which she researched, designed and built sets for, and cast. A two-volume account of the undertaking remains in the library there—to discourage other students from attempting the same.

After earning her degree she remained in San Francisco and did some freelance stage-managing for two or three companies that were trying to produce new kinds of theater forms. "It was all very academic and very much protest. Full of sound and fury and signifying nothing."

Then she started working for Gloria Unti's Performing Arts Workshop (PAW) in the predominantly black Fillmore district. Suddenly almost everyone she worked with, almost all of her friends, and all of her students were black. Skip had come from a long line of sharecroppers and migrant workers who had very definite attitudes toward blacks. "They were basically hardworking, poor whites. My father didn't rant and rave, but there was definitely a racial prejudice in my family." Growing up in southwest Kansas, where there were very few blacks, Skip did not absorb that attitude. She did not care who anybody was or what they were. But she was not prepared for the PAW either.

"There was a whole other culture that I had to be introduced to. A whole other language. These were not southern blacks either. These were urban blacks; they were really tough kids. None of them went to school. Most of them were on drugs."

About three hundred students participated in the year-round program that included classes, workshops, and performances. Skip started out as stage manager, later teaching acting classes and performing. When she left she was assistant director of the program. They did everything: theater, dance, mime; everywhere: in the streets, on a stage, at San Quentin; against terrible odds: poverty, drugs, thefts, staffing and funding problems. "It was a grand and glorious time, which was supported by the white liberals who had art galleries downtown and would come out once a year to the gym and drink champagne and watch the kids do a show, write us another check."

Though the majority of their financial support came from the Ford Foundation, the Arts Commission, and the National Endowment for the Arts, Skip saw the function of the PAW as more social than artistic. "The basic concept that you can use the arts in order to touch someone's life to make it a better place for that person to exist was set out there. And I think that's what I picked up more than anything else and brought back here."

Toward the end of the 1960s, after Martin Luther King, Jr. was killed, things started getting rough. Two armed Black Panthers had to escort Skip to her office. "I love the Black

Panthers. It was a tremendous group. The Panthers really helped that community, and they worked very well with us. I don't think we could have kept our place if it hadn't been for them." Eventually the workshop did have to move out of the ghetto into a white area.

Things were turning nasty elsewhere in San Francisco as well. "The peace and love and brotherhood thing was short lived—like a flame it burned that long." Skip snapped her fingers. "A lot of panhandling, only panhandling wasn't nice, friendly panhandling anymore. And the Haight became a really, really bad place. The last two or three times that I went down there it was like the Tenderloin of San Francisco, people lying on the streets and vomiting. I would see people on the streets that I had known for years but hadn't seen for awhile, and everything between their ears was just totally destroyed. I started getting hassled on the street, and our apartment was broken into. I couldn't go down and do the laundry without being worried that someone was going to accost me. I was ready to leave."

So was her husband, Vincent. Originally from Brooklyn, he had followed her to San Francisco after receiving his degree in architecture from the University of Oklahoma and found a good job as a building supervisor with a large firm. He was not being hassled on the street. But he was having to deal with other people's problems and contractors without getting any of the benefits of the artistic aspects of the job. For a while he and a friend tried to start a small office by working in the evenings. But as they did not have the manpower to even bid for a big job, that mostly meant remodeling their friends' kitchens.

"We had looked for a place to buy. Ye gods—you can't buy anything in northern California in the Bay area. I mean it's just not available—unless you're a shipping magnate or something like that. We had to make a decision: were we going to stay in San Francisco and live in an apartment all our lives, or were we going to do something else, move somewhere else, take a new direction?" Skip snuffed out a cigarette and lit a new one.

"I think there was one day that really did it. I had a little basenji puppy we had raised in the apartment. We'd take him out, and we'd put him on his leash, and we'd walk him around the block, or we'd take him to the park." She sighed. "We went out on a weekend, and we took the dog. And we said, 'We're going to take this little dog and let him run around and see that there's something else besides the sidewalk and that fireplug over there.' We drove all day long. We drove up the coast, and then we took Highway 101 back down, past San Francisco and down past San Jose, and then back up. We drove for eight hours looking for a nice grassy field. Well, they're all fenced off with 'No Trespassing' signs. Or you go to a beach and shoulder your way through the crowd." She laughed. "It was just crazy. And I said, 'This is ludicrous. Why are we living in a place like this?'"

In September, 1972, Skip returned to Kansas alone and lived in the basement of her parents' home, in Sublette. The plan was for her to find a steady job so that they would have a salary to depend on when Vince came out and tried to set up an office. They figured that might take a year or two. It was the worst winter of her life: the basement leaked, her car leaked, and job prospects were bleak at best.

Before coming out she had set up an interview with a small college in another area. They had written her a few letters and sounded interested. In the meantime, though, the college had switched hands. "And they believed that women should teach things like cooking. We didn't get along at all, to say the least." She laughed. "I knew my goose was cooked when they said that they thought men should build scenery because 'they was stronger.'"

Skip made the round of TV stations and other area colleges and businesses, did some substitute teaching, and finally landed a job in January keeping books for a feedlot. She did not know anything about it but said she would learn.

After several months things began to turn around for the Mancinis. An architect who had met Vince earlier asked when he was coming out. He had started his own office and had a job that was too big for him to handle alone—bigger than his friend's kitchen. Would he be interested in forming a partnership? The matter was settled by phone, and Vince started working before he even came out.

Skip's project took longer to establish. After she had worked as a bookkeeper for a few months, she saw an ad in the paper for a social worker and sent a résumé. Impressed with her credentials, Wheatland Youth Services called and asked if she would set up a program similar to the one in San Francisco. She would be working with "hostile teenagers" in Garden City.

Skip recalled the first night. "We had three very scared little white junior-high girls sitting there. We sat and talked for an hour-and-a-half, and I went home and thought, 'Well, that's the end of that. So much for hostile youth in Garden City, Kansas.'" Word apparently got out, though, in the next week. The second time they met, there sat the same three white girls—and seventeen Chicano drop-outs. "It got real exciting real fast."

She called the seventeen her Street Toughs. At first they met only one night a week. Gradually, though, they formed a dance and theater group called "We Got It Together" and started putting on performances.

They also saw a bit of the world beyond Garden City. One year they picked up corn left in the fields after harvest, talked a farmer into firing up his combine and shelling it, and drove it to the grain elevator, where Skip persuaded the people to give them a good price for it. They made enough money for nineteen of them—some who had never been outside Garden City—to go to Chicago for a week. "We rode subways, and we took the Loop at rush hour, and we went everywhere. We ate bagels and lox up at the top of the Sears Tower out on the observation deck. We went into the Stock Market Exchange, and I never told them what it was, and they all thought it was some kind of lunatic asylum. I loved it because everything we did was totally new to them—even getting on a train, ordering a sandwich—everything was new."

The program made dramatic—in both senses of the word—differences in the lives of several of Skip's students. One went on to stage-manage and teach improvisation for a mental health agency, in Kansas City; another was working on a Master's in child care, with an emphasis in theater, particularly mime; several were working or studying professional theater and dance; and two were dancing professionally. "I don't know that this would have happened with these kids if they hadn't had this experience here. Maybe with some of them it would, but not all of them."

Changes in funding sources over the years gave Skip the chance to expand her program into many areas. When Wheatland Youth Services lost its grant, her program was picked up by the YMCA for a couple of years. She added a children's theater class, and it took off. Then the Garden City Recreation Commission took over, and she started adult theater classes and seasonal community theater, as well as classes in dance, graphic arts and visual arts, and a foreign film series.

"The musical is in the fall. I do the musical in order to do the other things I want to do. We make money with the musical, and we're able to bankroll our next season and to partially fund the foreign film series. We're also able to offer class free to any child who can't afford it. Our classes are tremendously cheap. It works out to a nickel a class per kid."

The broadening support of her program changed the constituency of her classes, particularly those for younger people. "The Chicano kids were outsiders who wanted to be outsiders. They wanted their own close-knit group. The kids I have now are basically middle-class to lower-middle-class white kids who wish terribly that they could be head cheerleaders. And because they think they're too fat or they're too awkward or they're too ugly or their father doesn't make enough money in a big fancy job or whatever, they can't compete with what they call the 'socie' way of life. They're just kind of on the outside.

"But I'm not talking tutu studios here, you know. I won't teach that. I won't allow that to be offered in my program. I just cannot compromise myself to do that. I have a very strong feeling about children and movement and creativity. And I think one of the worst things we can do for young children is to make them wear nylon-net tutus and do the same shuffle-ball-change-step—especially when they're at that age where

they're so susceptible to conforming." In Skip's shows, kids
wore T-shirts and jeans and developed their own dances.

Skip paused and took a sip of coffee. "I offered a children's
choreography class last year, and I loved that class. It was
exciting and new, and everybody felt good about themselves.
I had a boy in the class, and he learned the principles of choreography and movement. I don't know. You can develop a
sense of self-assurance and self-pride in who you are, what
you are. And then maybe when you get to be fourteen or fifteen, and you find that the only way to get accepted into society is to be a cheerleader and you can't do the high jumps and
the splits in the air, you've got something to fall back on. And
you can say, 'That doesn't really matter that much. I don't really *need* to do that in order to *be* a productive, caring, thinking person.' "

Skip witnessed a similar opening up in some of her classes
for adults. She described one of the women's literature and
creative-writing classes that she taught, in a nearby county,
through the outreach program of Garden City Community College. "We were in this little library, and in the winter we didn't
have any heat for a while because the furnace was broken. So
everybody had to wear their coats. One night this woman—a
nice lady who played the piano for church—brought in a poem
she had written about how she felt when her husband came to
bed. And it just blew everybody away. And then the next week
another lady started bringing in all these poems about things
she had been feeling, and pretty soon it turned into a kind of
therapy thing. We had a whole cycle of sex poems."

"Wasn't there some sort of scandal connected with those
classes?"

"There was a lot of talk about those classes for a while
because one time I had seventeen women enrolled and three of
them got divorces that semester. But I don't think it was the
class. I think it would have happened anyway. They were all
young women who just couldn't cope, and most of them were
not from the area, or if they were from the area, they had gone
away to college. But the women who really opened up with

the classes, their whole families opened up. At the end of each course we would have a reading of our works or a discussion group if it was a literature class. These farmers would come in, set there in their boots and seed caps, and listen to Emily Dickinson and Edna St. Vincent Millay. It was just a tremendous experience."

Skip looked at a folder of blank forms (from two years earlier) lying on her desk. "That's the kind of teaching I like to do because I didn't have to keep attendance and who was tardy and all this stuff. These people just came because they wanted to be there. They couldn't wait to get there every week. It really did touch their lives."

"You'd never make it in a public school system."

"Oh, I knew that from the very beginning. I taught a summer course at Berkeley on how to motivate the hostile teenager in the classroom. Yet I'm not allowed to teach in a public school because I couldn't ever get through the education courses. My first year at OU, there were two girls right across the hall from me who were taking education courses. While I was doing calculus and quantitative analysis, they were playing 'Three Blind Mice' on a flutophone and getting a college degree for it. And I said I'd never, ever walk into the education *building*. And I didn't. I never set foot in it the whole time I was there. And everyone said, 'You're crazy. It's going to hold you back from getting a job.' And I said, 'Naah—if I had to take that job, I can pick cotton. My father did it, I can do it.' It works out. You make your own position.

"You know, when Vince and I first decided to come back here, all our friends said, 'Oh, you'll hate it, you'll think it's terrible back there. What are you going to do with yourselves? You'll be so bored.' And ever since we came back we haven't had any time at all. What you do, I'm firmly convinced," she said, refilling her coffee mug, "is you move into an area and you help create your own job. That's what I did. And that's what he did. You have to believe in yourself. It's not *where* you're at, it's what you do. I really believe that. I get tired of people who run this area down and say, 'Oh there's nothing going on here,' and 'I can't wait to leave,' and 'It's so borrrrring.' Well, basically, those people are boring. That's their problem. It's not that the area is boring. It's that they're lazy."

In the late 1960s, while Skip was living in San Francisco, center-pivot irrigation came to Sublette. That, along with the oil and gas near Satanta, made Haskell County the third wealthiest county per capita in the entire nation. I asked Skip what sort of changes she had noticed in the area upon coming back.

She described two pictures, a before and an after, of downtown Sublette. In the 1950s, when she was a girl and worked in her father's drugstore, she watched the farm families come in on Saturdays to do their shopping. Afterward they always stopped in to have a treat—an ice cream or a Coke or a limeade. Then the men would go out and sit on their Chevies that were angle-parked in front of the drugstore and talk about the weather and the crops, while the women would all pile inside one car and talk. Memories of the dust bowl and hard times were not far behind. They still had few luxuries and did much of their own work. "Make a nice Edward Hopper painting." Skip laughed gently. "I'm not one of these misguided liberals who say that poor people are beautiful. But there was some kind of a work ethic there, and there was some kind of a social tie—this was a big thing to go into town on Saturday. It was necessary that you maintain contact with your neighbors.

"Today in Haskell County people go to Dodge City or Garden to do the small shopping, and to Kansas City or Wichita or Denver or Dallas for the big purchases." An untaken photograph defined the new Haskell County for Skip. She saw it during the farm strike of 1976. The county strike office was located in a Western-wear boutique that had gone out of business. Skip walked out of her father's drugstore one day and saw this juxtaposition: the old Wild West storefront with "Daddy's Money" burned into wood across the top and an American Agricultural Movement Headquarters sign in the window underneath. The caption was provided when she went over and asked for one of the officials of the AAM, in Haskell County, and was told that he would not be back for three weeks—he had gone to Hawaii on vacation.

"Once I wrote a poem when I came back here about the prairie being like the ocean—because it was an ocean at one time. And I think it still is. But it takes a great deal of insight to see the beauty of this area. You have to look very closely—or you have to look very broadly. You have to stand way back and look at the scope of it. And maybe that's one reason why the kids in Haskell County that are now young farmers and ranchers don't have any identity or roots. They don't have a lake where they went fishing with their father when they were kids and that they took their girlfriends to when they were growing up or where they take their families now on weekends. There aren't any lakes. There aren't any trees. I guess that's what I was saying about the people in the fifties that used to sit on the cars. There was a ritual that is no longer there. I think rituals are very important to everybody's life. That's why the arts are very important—because they're basically rituals. They come from a long line of rituals, beginning with storytelling around a fire, dancing in circles."

Skip paused to sip some coffee and then looked up. "You know, before, I told you that it's not where you're at, it's what you do. But to a certain extent it is where I'm at here. Because when I came here there wasn't anything. It really is like virgin territory. I think it is really exciting to put on something—some kind of live, interacting performance—and have people come in who have never seen anything but Jaycee roller derby that's brought here from Wichita. To come into a theater and to see the lights and the sets, or just to see the bodies up there talking and responding to you is very exciting.

"We've done some fairly radical things on stage—not radical by California standards—but radical in terms of the area and the people here and what they've been exposed to." She mentioned her current production of *Cabaret*. "I'm staging it as Brechtian epic theater with a Greek chorus and projections and masks. It's going to be really interesting. We may have some theater riots because people like to see the guy get the girl, and they like to see cute patchwork quilts and all that kind of thing—which we've never given them. I mean I did do

Oklahoma, but we did it in a naturalistic style. We put dirt on the stage, and we had sweat. We took horse manure and spread it over everything so you could smell it."

"Don't you ever run out of ideas?"

Skip nodded. Earlier in the summer she had spent six weeks in Minneapolis observing a children's theater company. "I was just totally sapped out creatively. People had been sucking me dry for eight years. Every original idea that I ever even thought of, I had tried on stage. I needed to get away."

At other times during the year she made shorter trips, to California, New York, and Chicago, where she saturated herself with performances and exhibits and came back with fresh images for her own program. When she was really desperate to get away, she made a day trip to Wichita, over two hundred miles away, watched three movies, and turned around and drove back.

Skip was planning some changes in her program for the next year that she hoped would give her more time for travel and for free time at her home on the prairie. Designed by Vincent, "Prairie Swift" is decidedly modern: the outside features white-stained redwood, lots of glass, and an international architectural style. The inside is spacious with few doors or furnishings. A skylight provides sun for the trees and plants in one part. Located fifteen miles northwest of Sublette, the house was farther out than either had originally had in mind: both commuted seventy to eighty miles daily to and from Garden City. But it was the only place they could find.

"People come here from all over thinking they're going to find themselves an old house in the country with all this Victorian bric-a-brac—like the one in *Giant.* They're going to buy it and fix it up and get back to the fat of the land, like Lenny and George. Well, there aren't any old Victorian houses here. There never were. There wasn't any lumber. There were sod houses, and there were tents—those are hard to preserve. Are you going to find a piece of antique canvas or something and restore it? I mean, if they want to live in what people lived in, that's what they should do."

Skip laughed. Then her face grew determined again, and she pointed her cigarette at me. "I would like to do something exploring and exploding these myths of the West. If I ever get enough money, I'd like to go away and study how to make a film, and I'd like to make a film about feedlot cowboys. When I worked at the feedlot . . ."

CHAPTER 8

Jayhawks

FOR ABOUT AN HOUR ON A WEDNESDAY EVENING in October, 1982, it looked as if the city commission meeting in Garden City would never get under way. Two female reporters—one with blond, frizzy hair and the other with dark, frizzy hair—stood outside the door of the commission chamber, while men in blue suits, dark and light, milled about the front of the room discussing the difference between "effect" and "affect." " 'Affect' is when you do something to someone else," said one. He fetched a dictionary and read a definition aloud. By means of desk plates and name tags, I eventually sorted out the various city staff—the city attorney, city clerk, city manager, and assistant city manager. Only two of the five commissioners, however, were present. One commissioner was vacationing in Hawaii (pronounced "Ha WOY" by most of the people there); another, in the construction business, was late getting in his concrete and probably would not be coming; and Rodney Hoffman, the youngest commissioner, was speaking to a teachers' group and was expected shortly. Until Rodney arrived, there would be no quorum.

City commission meetings in Garden City are usually long, averaging about four and a half hours once a week, and are occasionally controversial. When a dispute flared between city and county law-enforcement officials during the spring of 1981, full-page transcripts of the meetings appeared in the newspaper. Recently united in a consolidated Law Enforcement Center, the officials had trouble agreeing on how they should talk to one another. Grover Craig, sheriff for as long as most people in Garden City could remember, thought they should use official 10-code for communicating over the radio; Police Chief Jerald Vaughn thought it made more sense to use plain speak. Neither would give in, and so they settled for a compromise: the county would use 10-code, and the city would use plain speak.

More often, city commission meetings consist of elaborate discussions about smaller, less heated matters—the color scheme for the park band shell ("White has always been good enough since I've lived here," grumbled Commissioner Duane West, who opposed both the three- and seven-color plans) or granting permission to an aspiring eleven-year-old entrepreneur to paint address numbers alongside curbs.

Sewers were the major topic of discussion the night I was there. They talked about PIs (points of intersection) and who owns what property and whether routing the sewer through there would upset their business. Mayor West (the mayor is selected by the commissioners on a yearly basis) displayed a remarkable knowledge of what seemed to be every road, business, and tree in the city. The reporters drifted in and out of the room, snacked on candy lozenges, and talked to one another. I doodled.

At 7:40 P.M., having given his report, the city manager—a short, white-haired man known for his long-winded mumble and infinite knowledge of Garden City—took off to pack for a trip. "Drive carefully," cautioned one of the blue suits. "Are you going to Hawaii, too?" asked one of the frizzy-haired reporters standing in the hall.

The discussion of routes and drainage ditches continued among the two commissioners and three other men who had come to present their plan. During a lull in the conversation one commissioner remarked that he was going to go to sleep if there was not more action.

At 8:10 P.M. the door below boomed shut, the noise echoing up the stairway to the chamber, followed by the sound of footsteps and a second door slamming shut. A lean, young man of medium height, wearing a dark-blue jacket, strode to the front of the room. "Sorry I'm late, Mr. Mayor. I was home watching the ball game, and my wife said, 'Hey, don't you have a city commission meeting tonight?' And I looked at my watch and said, 'By gosh, I do.'"

Rodney was joking about forgetting the meeting. Replacing the all-day commission meetings on alternate Mondays with weekly meetings every Wednesday night was the first action he took upon becoming mayor in 1979. Night meetings, he contended, would allow more people to attend or even run for the commission in the future. When one commissioner wondered how the city staff would be compensated for the night meetings, Rodney said they were professionals, and night meetings would be considered part of their job. On the following Wednesday the Commission held its first night meeting in thirty years. About thirty-five people attended.

Rodney had filed for the city commission only a few months earlier—minutes before the noon deadline. The youngest commissioner then was in his late thirties; the median age in Garden City was twenty-six; Rodney was twenty-five.

His experience as a reporter for the *Garden City Telegram* and as assistant manager of a farm-related business had given him the confidence and knowledge to take on a more public role. "Gosh, I've lived in Garden City, I'm familiar with these issues. And I see now that you don't have to have a law degree or be the financial chairman of your company to be able to run something. It just takes people with common sense, dedication, and the ability to work with other people on these things."

The closest Rodney had come to political office before was in high school, when he performed a scene from *Julius Caesar:*

Let me have about me men that are fat;
Sleek-headed men, and such as sleep o'nights:
Yond Cassius has a lean and hungry look;
He thinks too much: such men are dangerous.

[1.2.192–95]

To achieve the proper tenseness in his voice, he practiced in the snow; he performed in a toga.

His campaign picture for the commission was more casual. He stood out on the highway in a sweat jacket, wind blowing his hair, grain elevators in the background. His campaign was low key, self-effacing: "I'm not saying I'm the best candidate for the job (too often the best candidates don't get involved). I am saying that my journalistic and business background has given me the chance to listen to a wide range of people, and I don't intend to ignore that if elected." Friends and relatives (he has close to a hundred first cousins, many of whom live in the area), advertising, and lots of door-to-door campaigning placed him third in a field of ten candidates in the primary, held six weeks after he filed.

On April 3 an unseasonable two inches of snow fell on Garden City, and 53 percent of the registered voters (up from 32 percent in 1977) turned out to vote in the general election. Rodney received 2,793 votes, which made him the top vote-getter and youngest commissioner ever. The first runner-up was some seven hundred votes behind. Two incumbents were voted out of office, and another came in a distant third. Garnering the most votes gave Rodney a four-year term as commissioner and the probability of being mayor the first year, subject to confirmation by the other commissioners.

A week later he took the mayor's seat for the first time. "This seat isn't as hot as I thought it would be," he said. "You just haven't been there long enough," replied a veteran commissioner.

So far during his stint on the commission, Rodney had often found himself in the minority. A historical preservation ordinance he had supported failed to pass, most commissioners feeling that that sort of thing should be handled by the private sector: If they want to tear it down, that's fine. We shouldn't be able to tell them that they can't tear it down just because it's old. He was the only one to oppose a public auction of guns confiscated by the police department. And always there was a struggle to persuade the more conservative commissioners to spend available money. In September, 1982, for instance, the city staff presented a community development block grant application asking HUD for $488,000. Duane West, perhaps the most frugal of the commissioners, spoke against it: it was exactly such handouts that had put the federal government in the red in the first place. He convinced another commissioner of his view, and, along with the absence of still another, the proposal failed two-to-two.

Rodney had his victories as well. He persuaded the commissioners to have the city fund a series of free concerts in Stevens Park during the summer of 1982. And earlier he had worked with them to persuade voters to pass a half-cent city sales tax to pay for new services and buildings necessitated by the growth of the city, including the city administration hall in which their meetings were held. In 1975 the voters turned down the tax by a nine-to-one majority, but in 1981, when Rodney was on the commission, they passed it seven-to-three.

Watching Rodney at the meeting in October, I was reminded more of George Gibbs or George Willard than of a lean and plotting Roman. Grinning, he walked over to the large city map on an easel and pointed out his suggestions for the routing of the sewer. He talked easily, eagerly—as if he had been discussing sewers and drainage ditches all his life.

Not a politician but a priest was what I originally had Rodney figured for. During his freshman year of high school he left home to attend the Precious Blood Fathers Seminary, just outside of Kansas City. His younger sister and I were excited: we were finally going to witness a metamorphosis from the secular to the religious life.

Catholicism runs deep in Rodney's family. His paternal ancestors, Volga Germans, came to Kansas from Russia in 1908 to escape religious persecution. They settled in central Kansas, near the town of Emmeram, a settlement of no more than twenty houses, a grocery store, and a Catholic Church. Rodney's great-grandfather built a house in town just so the family would have a place to stay between the morning and evening services on Sunday, when they came in from the farm.

While still in his early teens, Rodney's father, one of thirteen children, left the family farm to attend a Catholic boys' high school in Hays, Kansas. Though he never finished, he felt his time there had been valuable.

When I talked with him in 1982, Rodney remembered his own Catholic education with a similar sense of gratitude. "For me a couple of good things came of it," he said, referring to his eight years at Saint Mary's, in Garden City. His voice was soft, slow, deliberate. "For one, there was some good discipline, and that came from the nuns. We seemed to be able to move through a lot of material even though it was an awful large class—thirty to thirty-five students. And there was a lot of homework, so I developed some good study habits." He cited the reputation of Saint Mary's students for being scholastically superior to their public-school counterparts when they joined them in high school.

At the seminary Rodney found an even more stringent education. Classes were smaller—nineteen his freshman year, fourteen or fifteen his sophomore year—and the course load heavier: French, Latin, biology, geometry, religion, history, and English. Two hours a night, six nights a week, they had a mandatory study hall. He found the atmosphere a bit stifling.

"There you begin to talk a little bit more about being in a closed system. The first year I was there they didn't even allow transistor radios. Everybody had them, but they didn't allow them."

"Is that why you left?"

Rodney nodded. "Because it was four hundred miles away from home, I only saw my family at Christmas and Easter. I got into Kansas City maybe once a month. But there wasn't a lot of social interaction or new people. I felt I was missing out on a lot. And, of course, there was this natural curiosity about the other sex. I just felt that, hey, if you are going to be celibate, you'd better understand this natural tendency towards the other sex."

That curiosity touched upon an old fear that his mother, also of staunch German Catholic stock, harbored. According to a local story, shortly after Rodney was born she ran into an acquaintance who congratulated her on her firstborn. "Thank you," she said nervously, "but what if he grows up to marry someone who isn't a Catholic?"

When he returned to Garden City his junior year to finish up at the public high school, Rodney ran the risk of meeting Protestant females. He found the academic standards somewhat lax and didn't play varsity sports, so he took up drama, where the teachers were willing to spend extra time with students. His senior year, while working on the children's play, *The Dragon That Giggled,* he met Barbara Nelson, a sophomore and a Lutheran.

Barb laughed when I mentioned the story about Mrs. Hoffman to her. Slight, blond, and of Norwegian descent, she spoke with less reserve and reverence than Rodney—with a sort of sunny sarcasm.

"We had a priest at our wedding, the kids are Catholic. But you see, I'm real stubborn. There's no way I'd ever convert."

"How did you get mixed up with drama in high school?"

"I think when I first started it was just something else. I was in everything. You should see the list after my name in the yearbook—Kayettes, FHA, Pep Club . . . I was Miss All-American. But then after awhile the drama group became a sort of family, a security thing. That was your little group of friends. It was a lot different from my other group of friends—I mean I had football players as boyfriends. It was a real evolution for me. I think it made me grow up—or try to grow up—very quickly."

In January of her senior year Barb became one of the first students to graduate early. "I thought Garden City was pretty repressive. I couldn't wait to get out."

The death of her father that spring and concern for her mother, however, kept her in Garden City through the next fall. She attended the local community college and acted in a few plays. The following January, at last, she headed for the University of Kansas, in Lawrence.

A "JAYHAWKS" license tag on the back of one car and a tag with a picture of the bird on the front of another declared both Barb's and Rodney's affection for their alma mater. The mascot of KU, the fictitious bird (a cross between a bluejay and a hawk) has its origins in the mid-nineteenth century. The term "jayhawkers" was used variously to refer to a company of gold seekers on their way to California and then to a band of guerrillas in Kansas, initially antislavery men, who conducted raids into Missouri before and during the Civil War. Later the name was applied to all Kansans and then more specifically to students at the University of Kansas who adopted the marauding bird as their symbol.

"We just had a wonderful time," said Barb, her legs tucked underneath her. "We would go to Kansas City and go out to eat, see a movie, and do a lot of things. You know, when we left Garden City, that was a one-movie and two-restaurant time."

"What about your classes?"

"Kind of a novelty. I really enjoyed a little bit more pressure. I'm not a super-competitive person, but when I got an 'A' in my little blue book, it really meant a lot, whereas in high school, it didn't. I remember some of the people who graduated with high honors from high school. It was just a joke because they'd taken rug-hooking and elementary ed. assistant, all that stuff."

At KU Barb studied mostly social history, an interest sparked by her father's concern with history and a high-school class in which she'd done research on Japanese relocation camps. Knowing that she had to have some marketable skill, she decided to be a history teacher.

Barb laughed and shook her head. "Little did I know there were absolutely no jobs, especially for someone who couldn't coach. I should have known, coming from the high school here in Garden City. Of course I didn't know that went on everywhere—at least in Kansas."

Barb also was not prepared for the bias against people from western Kansas. It was perhaps worst at Shawnee Mission, a middle- to upper-middle-class suburb, where she did her student teaching. " 'All farmers are dense,' 'Western Kansas is cold'—I was just amazed at the generalizations they came up with. They haven't seen anything in western Kansas except Goodland because that's on the interstate on the way to Colorado."

The year before Barb did her student teaching, she and Rodney had married. He graduated at the end of that year and interned at the *Garden City Telegram* over the summer. They offered him a job, so after Barb finished her student teaching in December, 1976, the Jayhawks moved back to Garden City, somewhat reluctantly.

"I really liked living in Kansas City. But then I can't say honestly that I would have stayed there, even if Rodney hadn't gotten the job. I couldn't even get a substitute teaching job there."

In Garden City Barb easily found a job substituting at the high school, but establishing her credibility with veteran teachers there proved harder. One of her first days back she was walking down the hall after the bell had rung when her speech teacher of a few years before accosted her. "What are you doing in the hall? Why aren't you in class?" he bellowed at her. She looked at him. He looked at her. "My God, you're back! I feel so old." Later in the teachers' lounge he told another former teacher of hers about the encounter. "Look at that. She's already done with school." "Who cares?" said the other. "She still looks like she's fifteen."

She may have looked fifteen, but at twenty-one, Barb's responsibilities had increased considerably. Both of her parents were dead, her mother having died while she was at KU. And shortly after returning to Garden City, she found out that she and Rodney were going to become parents.

"I always blamed that on Garden City," said Barb, laughing. "I came back and zap!"

Seth was born the next September, followed by Sean two years later. Barb knew she could not spend all her time at home. "I have a lot of friends that don't work, that do absolutely all the child care and all the housework. I'm amazed, because I just can't do that. It would wreak havoc on me. I have to work or at least go to school."

While she still had her stitches from Seth's childbirth, Barb started taking telenetwork courses. She did some substitute teaching and worked part time at a day-care center for mentally and physically handicapped children. "Moving back here there aren't a lot of educational opportunities. You can take nursing. Well, I already had four years of college. I wanted to build on that and not start all over. I thought about going into elementary education because I probably would have had a pretty good chance of getting an elementary position. But it was just *too* traditional. I had to do something a little different."

Barb ended up working with students who are different, the learning disabled. At the elementary level, several teachers in Garden City had specializations in learning disabilities, but at the secondary level, Barb found it was pretty much untrod territory. She took enough courses to become provisionally certified and drove across the state visiting programs.

Though few in number—from two to five in each class—her students had a wide range of abilities. "I've got some really good math students and some that are really terrible. Some can't read 'The cat is black,' and others can read just fine. Legally you have to develop an IEP: Individual Educational Program. There are a lot of people who say you shouldn't do tutorials because they're not long range, they won't cure anything. And I can see that. But then that doesn't help much when kids are flunking out of school. So I've tried to hit the balance: keeping them passing their classes and then working on some study skills or survival skills, depending on the student. I don't like tracking kids. I try to encourage as many as I can to go on to college. But it's amazing what some of them don't know—what country they live in, how to tell time. It's scary."

The front screen door slammed shut, and Seth, almost five, and Sean, almost three, charged through the house with friends.

Barb smiled. "Working, not working—that's been a big issue with me. I don't know if you ever settle it. Last year I felt rotten because I worked full time. I don't care what people say, I still swear these kids suffer. I don't believe in quality time. They just want me around, they want me here. They made that perfectly clear. It's a lot easier to leave a little baby than a very verbal four- or five-year-old who can tell you, 'I don't want you to go. I want you to stay home.' "

Working also cut into Barb's volunteer activities. In her first years back she worked with the March of Dimes and later served a stint as president of the Friends of the Library board. "I've kind of dropped in causes. Like community theater—I was so involved with that. I directed two plays when I was pregnant with Seth; even after he was born, I acted in one. I taught a course at the Juco (Garden City Community Junior College) in theater. That was something I had to give up. There are a lot of things I'm putting on the back burner. I just really want to spend a lot of time with my kids now. Let some other people do the volunteering for awhile. You get burned out. I'm narrowing." She laughed.

While Barb and Rodney were making adjustments to their new responsibilities, Garden City was undergoing its own growing pains. New industry and prosperity brought in young people from surrounding towns and other states and attracted back people Barb and Rodney had gone to school with. Rodney's ten-year high-school reunion, class of 1971, revealed that half of the three hundred members of his class lived in Garden City.

"Do you think the people here are more conservative than elsewhere?"

Barb tilted her head, considering the question. "I really don't think it's as oppressive as some people think—or like to think—it is. You get quite a cross section in Garden City. There's no segregation: there's one high school, everybody goes to it. I think that was a real interesting revelation for me, realizing that bigger wasn't necessarily better. At Shawnee Mission, where I taught, there was no diversity—the kids were all middle to upper-middle class, and they were a lot more bigotted than we ever were."

Housing in Garden City, on the other hand, had become more segregated than when she was a child. "That's what I kind of hate to see about Garden. You used to see a rather modest home next to a nice home, and now yours has got to be like everybody else's on the block. If you live here, you're lower- to middle-middle class; if you live here, you're middle class; and if you live here, you're definitely lower class."

The response of many long-time Garden Citians to the recent influx of Vietnamese also disturbed Barb. "If I could give one reason in just the last few weeks for wanting to move, it's that I'm sick of hearing people complain about the Vietnamese. I'm just sick of it."

"Would you like to move?"

Barb shrugged. "I'm ambivalent. I love the city, I miss a lot of things—the restaurants, the movies . . . this, that, and the other. I really enjoyed visiting Escondido, California, this summer, but I can't imagine really living there. Maybe I'd like it. I'm kind of flexible—I adapted here just fine." She laughed. "I don't think I'd be one to move East. I haven't been there enough to say, really—I mean my idea of the East is Paramus, New Jersey. And I don't really have a burning desire to move to Denver, like everyone else seems to. I'm not convinced I need to move. It's not a big pressure. I could stay here—as long as I get to go on vacations."

"Ah criminy," said Rodney, when I asked him what he missed about KU. "I miss the library, the bookstores, the open exchange of ideas, the information, the variety of people you come in contact with, the scenery, the water—I like KU." Dressed in a striped shirt and jeans, he leaned back in a kitchen chair and grinned. "The Athens on the Kaw."

The mood of protest had pretty well died out by the time Rodney made the seven-hour drive across the state to hillier, greener, wetter country. There were a few students with long hair, but the most vocal protesters were Iranians. Linda Lovelace was on campus to make a movie. Streakers appeared in the spring. Sororities and fraternities were beginning to regain some of their former popularity. And Watergate was soon at its height, bringing to the fore a new idol for students: the investigative journalist.

Rodney was among those swept up in the media mania, but

for more traditional reasons. "Not so much because of the investigative aspects of the work but just because of the general fount of information you can find there. I can read newspapers like I read novels."

Good, clean copy editing, technically proficient style as well as a personal style, and covering all angles and doing so fairly were the skills he developed at the William Allen White School of Journalism. The autobiography of its namesake was one of the books that stood out in Rodney's memories of those years. "I learned a lot about people, a lot about Kansas, Kansas politics—he ran for governor, you know—a lot about small-town journalism, always one of my interests."

Rodney wrapped his Nikes around the chair legs. "Two teachers there will stand out forever in my mind, and, of course, they would stand out for anyone who's taken journalism there. One was Calder Pickett, a historian and journalist. My class with him was like no other class I've ever taken. He brought in a wealth of outside materials—records, film presentations, books, magazine articles—and sat you down for a fifty- or fifty-five-minute period and just poured out information from beginning to end. There was no way you could absorb it all. I think everyone always hated to see those lecture periods end.

"The other teacher was John Bremner, who taught copy editing. He's the kind of guy that writes book reviews of dictionaries because he knows the dictionary better than American Heritage. The first thing he told us is that a journalist, particularly a copy editor, needs to be a Univac, able to assimilate a thousand pieces of information and store them for later use. He was a very forceful person in the classroom. He kept us on our toes—you couldn't sit back and expect him to lecture while you took notes."

"Was it difficult for you to move back to Garden City?"

Rodney paused a moment before answering. "Not really. I had worked as an intern at the *Telegram*, so I was able to move into that job somewhat easily. At the same time, the town had grown so much since I'd graduated from high school that in a lot of respects, even though the turf was the same, there were a lot of things I didn't know about Garden City. In some regards it was like moving to a strange town."

Working for a large newspaper had been one of Rodney's goals in college; but with new mouths to feed, he thought he had better find a more lucrative job. After working for eighteen months at the *Telegram*, he quit to become assistant manager of Standard Supply, a farm-supply store that Barb's father had owned and where both of her brothers worked.

Being a downtown merchant required Rodney to work six days a week and in some ways was more confining. "I certainly had a less-structured workday at the newspaper, in some respects. A lot of times I was left to my own initiative to develop my assignments. It wasn't, 'Go do this today,' 'Go do that tomorrow,' and 'Have this done by the end of the week.' It was more, 'What are you going to do for us today?' 'What are you going to do for us by the end of the week?'"

Working in a business dependent on the agricultural industry, Rodney found, did provide its own challenges and education. "Trying to outguess the farm economy, trying to outguess the farmer, trying to outguess the economy in general is part of my job. I find farmers fascinating. They've got to do so many things. One day they're plumbers, and the next day they're electricians, and the next day they're mechanics, and the next day they're inventors, and the next day they're commodities experts, trying to figure out whether to buy or sell, and the next day they're gardeners, trying to figure out why their crop is not growing or what that bug is there, and the next day they're businessmen at the bank trying to borrow money, trying to pay off loans. It's a terribly complex job."

"Some people say that the local economy, based as it is on irrigation, is a false one. That it's doomed to collapse because of the limited supply of water. What do you think?"

Rodney winced and said softly, "I think there's probably a lot of truth in that." He paused. "But it seems not uncommon. The entire economy of the country is based on a lot of that kind of falseness, whether you're selling cars or television sets or things that are built to last a year or two or three years and not to last a lifetime or even twenty years. And that's the mentality we've got. I guess it's only natural that it would happen here too. There is certainly some question as to how much—or even whether—farming should be done in parts of western Kansas, eastern Colorado, shortgrass areas. I don't know that they shouldn't have been left that way."

He mentioned a trip that he, his sons, and his father took to see his grandfather's homestead in central Kansas, where his ancestors had discovered the futility of farming. At one time some of the ground had been broken out into cropland, but it was eventually turned back into grassland when they discovered it was not worth farming. The house had long since been moved into the town of Victoria, but an L-shaped arrangement of irises still grew where two sides of the house had been.

A sadness slipped into Rodney's tone as he talked about the Arkansas River, one of his fascinations as a child that he was not able to share with his sons. "They say that a weed—the salt cedar tree—now will take over the river. The darn thing grows and just takes over everything. You could hardly crawl through it if you got down on your stomach. Its leaves have kind of a salty taste, and when they drop, they sterilize the soil so that nothing else can grow. It's not a pretty picture."

Becoming a city father made Rodney more aware of the welfare of his hometown, of the complex balance between nature and human ambition; becoming a father made him more aware of the welfare of his family, of the sometimes precarious balance between life and death. Both Seth and Sean had problems with allergies, and Seth had been in the hospital with respiratory problems. "I didn't think my mom and dad ever thought about our health that much. But gosh, they seem so fragile. And they're not. They're tough. They can take falls and scrapes and a thousand other things. But we have had a little bit of serious concern about the allergies."

Rodney looked at the cookies that his mother had sent over for his birthday. "I like to think I look ahead and think about my family's future. But at the same time I look back and I see the years going by and, my gosh, where are they going? I can't believe I'm actually growing older. I just assumed I would stay eighteen or twenty forever. I never imagined myself when I was in high school or even college being a part of a family at this particular age—I'm twenty-nine now. My dad was thirty-six when he got married, and I always told everyone, 'Well, I'm going to wait until I'm thirty-six.' And yet this happened, and it's been tremendous."

"What do you see down the road for yourself and your family in, say, ten years?"

Rodney smiled and shook his head. "Right now I can't see past November 2. I really can't."

November 2 was the date for the general election. Rodney was running for the state legislature. Again it was a late decision. Late in August he was drafted by the local Democrats, though friends said he had the bug. It was turning out to be a heartbreaker of a race. His opponent was a popular Republican incumbent with fourteen years behind him, who ran for the first time when he was in law school. There were no issues and certainly no arguments ad hominem. Both could win prizes for politeness. Every door in the city had been knocked on at least twice, and the battle of the yard signs was dividing neighbor from neighbor.

He did not say, but perhaps more long-range political ambitions were in the back of Rodney's mind when he mentioned that he would like to spend a year or two or three in Washington, D.C., to expose the boys to a different atmosphere. For the time being, though, they settled for trips to South Dakota to visit Barb's relatives, to California, and to Colorado.

Rodney grinned. "One of my campaign promises was to move the city to the mountains."

CHAPTER 9

South of the Tracks

"YOU CAN DO ANYTHING YOU WANT TO DO. But you can't work hard at it. You can't get by just by working hard at it. You can't be good, you have to be twice as good. Because if you're not, they won't let you play. Because you're a Mexican."

The subject at the time was baseball. But for Dennis Garcia, thirty-one-year-old managing attorney for Kansas Rural Legal Services, in Garden City and Dodge City, his father's words became a code of life.

"Now that I look back at it, I don't know if that was right or not," he said, relaxing in the home in which he and his nine siblings grew up. "It made me almost paranoid about who I was. I was too concerned about what I was."

The small, white, frame house that Dennis's parents had lived in since the day they were married is located between the grain elevators and the zoo, in Garden City, on the wrong side of the tracks. Once known as Little Mexico, this area housed Mexican-Americans when they first started coming to Garden City from Mexico and Texas in the early 1900s to work on the railroad. Actually it consisted of two neighborhoods—a fact little known outside the Hispanic community until early in 1982 when the Finney County Historical Museum featured the community in an exhibit. Those living west of Main Street were called la Nalga, Spanish for "buttock," because of a Mexican madame who ran a brothel there in the 1890s. Those on the east side, where the women were noted for gossiping, were known as la Garra, from the Spanish expression "sacando la garra" (chewing the rag). When Dennis was growing up, they were referred to simply as West-siders and East-siders.

Dennis's paternal relatives crossed the border into El Paso in 1911. They followed the Santa Fe Railroad until they reached Holcomb, just west of Garden City. Dennis's father, D. C., was born in 1922, and shortly thereafter the family moved to a house on the corner of Fourth Street, east of Main, south of the tracks. Besides the Garcias, there were three other main families on the East side: the Mesas, the Guillens, and the Valenzuelas. Among them they had thirty-six children.

The offspring of those children provided Dennis with many playmates while he was growing up. And as the oldest of three boys, with seven sisters (four older and three younger than he was) to do the household chores, he had plenty of free time. "I had it made."

Baseball was their game. They usually played just in their neighborhood, but occasionally they crossed Main Street to play the West-siders. That made Dennis a little nervous, but he could still play.

Crossing the tracks was a different ball game altogether. He remembered the first time he played baseball at a city recreation program. "Frightened out of my wits: I knew no one, I was the only Mexican. I just remember being so nervous that I couldn't play, that no one had confidence in me that I could perform, that I could play." His father's words only made him more self-conscious.

Gradually, though, they became his fuel and sports his road to gaining acceptance beyond the tracks. "As a child I wanted to be accepted more than anything—accepted outside of the family. And I found out early that one of the best ways to do that is to be successful in sports." His white classmates at Saint Mary's began to notice and respect Dennis's skill in sports. They started crossing the tracks to his neighborhood to play ball, and sometimes they played in municipal programs on the other side of the tracks. "If I had plenty of guys who went to school with me at Saint Mary's, I was okay."

He sought out his own sports heroes. In fourth grade he noticed a good high-school football player, who was black, and asked for his autograph. He was Mike Johnson, who later played alongside Gale Sayers at KU and became a pro for the Dallas Cowboys. Dennis smiled. "Bet you I was the first kid who asked that guy for his autograph."

I pointed at three baseball trophies on top of the television set in the corner. "Yours?"

Dennis nodded. "Funny thing about those trophies is they've all come in the last two years—from playing in city leagues and tournaments." He chuckled. "I played all my life and most of the time fairly well—not excellent, but very well. And I'd been on winning teams. But I'd never won an individual trophy. My younger brothers were in track, and they'd won medals, and they all had their individual trophies. I was beginning to think I would play all those years and believe myself to be very good, and I wouldn't have anything to show for it."

"So now it's paying off?"

"Now it's paying off." He laughed. "Many years later my parents' TV is adorned with three trophies."

In fifth and sixth grades, sports were tied to grades. Boys who wanted to play basketball had to maintain a certain grade-point average every week. Dennis's teacher determined he was an "A" student.

"I had to play, so I studied. Not to be smart—Lord knows to this day I hate studying—but it was a way to get what I wanted. I guess I learned the old carrot-and-stick thing pretty good, you know. If I did this, I'll be accepted. I'll be okay."

Academically, Dennis had a head start over some of the other Mexican-Americans: English was his native language. Both of his parents were native Spanish speakers, their mothers being born in El Paso and their fathers in the central part of Mexico. Speaking only Spanish and missing school several weeks at a time because of seasonal work in the sugar-beet fields meant that few of the children succeeded in school. Dennis's mother, Irene, was an exception: one of two Hispanics in her class to graduate from high school, in Dodge City. More often they dropped out in eighth grade, as D. C. did, to start working full time. Only recently did D. C. earn his General Equivalency Diploma (G.E.D.). When he was elected mayor of Garden City in 1974, Irene often served as his ghostwriter. To prevent their children from having to suffer the same difficulties in school, they decided to speak English in the house once they were married.

In seventh and eighth grades Dennis lettered on Saint Mary's basketball team. "I played real hard. I played with intensity—the words they use now are 'reckless abandon.' I just gave it hell because I believed what my father told me. And he was right. When I played sports, they took notice."

One nun who noticed pulled him aside after a game and told him, "If you would try as hard in your studies as you do on the basketball court, you could do anything you wanted."

Her words, perhaps, were what encouraged him to become one of four boys in his class to sign up for the Precious Blood Father's Seminary in ninth grade. As a server for many Masses, Dennis knew immediately when a priest made a mistake and had often practiced saying the Mass himself when he was younger. He felt he qualified.

For his mother, the seminary was the best thing that ever happened to him. At Saint Mary's Dennis had been rebellious: he could count on getting F's in conduct. When he came back from the seminary, he was calmer, less rambunctious.

"You want to know what *I* remember most about the seminary? Three square meals a day. Three square meals a day. I couldn't believe it." Dennis laughed. "I gained twenty-five pounds that first year. You know we had a very staple diet at home. We always had plenty, but it was always beans and rice and eggs. My father got paid twice a month, and the day after, my mother would buy groceries. So twice a month, on Thursdays, we had hamburgers and pie. And if you missed that meal because you were gone or sick, you didn't get hamburger but once that month."

The next fall he was the only one of the four to return to the seminary. He stayed only a semester. "The summer after my first year at the seminary I had my first experience with the young ladies. I just remember kissing these young girls, and I thought it was terrific." That, along with the prospect of playing football, lured him back to Garden City.

The self-consciousness and shyness of his early days also returned. At Saint Mary's he had grown confident in his abilities and comfortable with his classmates. There had been a few rude reminders of his brown skin, but overall he felt that he was treated fairly. When he started at the public high school midway through his sophomore year, though, he found that the old Saint Mary's crowd had disappeared into the presiding social hierarchy of the public-school kids. He was once again the poor, unknown Mexican.

Racism in Garden City, Dennis suggested, was usually more a matter of slight than fight. "I don't think that it was the horrifying racism that you found in the deep South, with hangings and burnings and things like that. Or the ghettos of the North. But there were the personal insults and things that you would have to go through. For years only one barber in town would cut hair for Mexican males." During World War II his mother stood in line, pregnant, waiting for the rationed sheets and pillowcases and was passed over for three or four white women. His older sisters had to sit in the balcony of the movie theater. After World War II Dennis's father and other Mexican-American veterans came back and started demanding their rights. Most of the overt barriers to Mexican-Americans came down then. Still, the two volumes of Finney County history, published in the 1950s, contain no stories or pictures of Mexican-Americans, even though a few blacks—who constituted a smaller minority—are included.

A similar lack of recorded history bothered Dennis when he first started playing football. His junior year he made the B-team. He enjoyed playing, but the coaches did not know him. He had not played in junior high or his sophomore year. When he suited up for the first time, he had to watch the other players to make sure he got the pads in the right place. In the first game he was one of two juniors left behind. But the next week he played well during practice, blocking some extra points.

One coach noticed and put him in at the end of the first half of the next home game. He played well, and from then on the coach backed him.

Basketball was another story. Tryouts were on a Tuesday. Dennis did not have any tennis shoes. He told the coach that he would have to wait until Thursday, when he was paid from his part-time job. The coach told him that if he could not come out Tuesday not to come at all. Dennis got a little hot and stayed away. Later he got his revenge. "The very last nine weeks of my senior year I had to have a quarter credit of P.E. to graduate, and so I took an advanced P.E. course. This very same coach taught it, and we played basketball every day. After watching me play, he called me aside and said, 'Why in the world didn't you go out for basketball? I'm sure you could have made one of the teams.' 'Coach, if I tell you, you won't believe me.'" Dennis told him anyway, and the coach did not believe him.

Being Mexican and a jock put Dennis in a peculiar position socially. Most of the other Mexicans were doing other things—getting into trouble, drinking beer. As a jock, Dennis had to refrain. But he was not popular like the other jocks either. He was shy with women, particularly whites, and had only three or four dates all through high school.

"Plus I worked. After my sophomore year I went to work that summer. I began to realize then that my parents were not going to be able to put me through college. I would probably not get a full-ride scholarship somewhere. I would probably not get an athletic scholarship. So I had to plan on working and paying my way." Working part time and being on the football team, he had little time for other school activities. A classmate from Saint Mary's had to nudge him in class when he fell asleep.

"Was going to college your own idea?"

Dennis nodded. "The summer after the eighth grade at Saint Mary's my father took us out to work in the beet fields, hoeing beets. It was hot. We went out at sunrise and didn't come back until sunset. I couldn't get back in time to practice with the baseball team. I'd come back and practice after work in the fields, all alone. I was very tired. I remember making up my mind in the middle of one of those rows: 'I am going to college. I am not going to do this.' And that's what happened."

Soon after his senior year started he began counting the days until he could leave home. Albuquerque, where one of his sisters lived, and the University of New Mexico were his destination. At eight o'clock on a Wednesday night in May, 1969, he graduated from high school; by ten the next morning he was on his way to New Mexico with two boxes, $1,000 he had saved, and one of the first two scholarships awarded by the G.I. Forum.

Dennis's grades his first semester were a disaster: a 1.3 on a 4.0 scale. He dropped out and worked for a semester. The next fall he reenrolled, and his grades never again dropped below a 3.0.

During the intervening summer he returned home and worked at a gas station. Sometimes a girl he had called "Eyes" in high school came in with her boyfriend. He had wanted to ask her out when he was in high school, but he was too timid, afraid she would not go out with someone like him—a Mexican. One of his co-workers at the station told him that she had been interested in him until she had met the guy she was dating then.

"I began to realize then that I had sold myself short. I was too paranoid about who I was and what I was—and partly because of my dad's always telling me, 'You're not good enough like you are. You have to be twice as good.' "

In New Mexico his self-image changed. He was around a lot more Hispanics. They were everywhere—in banks, in politics, in education. There were school buildings and streets named after Hispanics. For the first time he was one of the masses. He did not stick out. "It was like being in heaven. Anglo kids, Anglo women having no fear at all just to come right up and talk to you, never feeling ashamed about being a Mexican. It was great."

Working at a gas station in Albuquerque the next summer, Dennis was a new person. He shunned the long sleeves and hat that he usually wore to prevent his skin from getting darker. The New Mexico sun burned him until he turned purple. He recalled a female customer asking him hesitantly if he was from India. " 'No, I'm a Chicano from Kansas,' I told her, but I was a little complimented. That's when I think I started getting rid of that phobia about being dark, about being Mexican."

In the spring of his senior year of college he married a woman from Mexico. In June, after graduating with a degree in business, he went to work for Sears.

"Sears, the world's number-one retailer. That's middle class, that's American." Dennis smiled. "I mean the only thing more American would probably have been IBM."

Ironically, Sears completed Dennis's cultural education. He spent ten months in a training program in Amarillo, learning all the divisions, paper flow through, audit control, and inventory. Then he was sent down to McAllen, Texas, right on the border, fifty miles west of Brownsville, to be in charge of a shoe department.

"And lo and behold, I get down there and 80 percent of my customers speak Spanish. So here I am—well educated, I thought, well rounded, ready to tear up the big corporate world as a success—and I can't begin to sell a pair of shoes," he paused and softened his voice, "because I don't know how to ask them what size, what color in the language. All this education I had—at that time eighteen years' worth—couldn't get me past a pair of tennis shoes."

Dennis's color only added to his embarrassment: customers assumed he spoke Spanish. But after hearing him struggle through a reply, they would say, "Usted no es de aquí" ("You're not from here").

Dennis began the slow, arduous task of learning the language of his ancestors. Fortunately he already had the vocabulary, having listened to his parents argue and his grandmother talk. But he did not know how to put the words together, how to change tenses. Within six months he was speaking Spanish 60 percent of the time; after a year about 80 to 85 percent of the time. "And I was a big success." He flashed a smile. "I don't want to say this bragging-wise, but my shoe department went from twenty-third out of twenty-seven stores to first, in about eight months." It was grossing $140,000 when he took over and $240,000 when he left.

Congratulations came from the Chicago buyer, who called Dennis long-distance when he was at a meeting one day. That was nice, he thought, but too bad it had not come from a little closer to home. His store manager had been mistreating him some. Success did not mean much, he decided, without the support of his immediate supervisor. He felt vulnerable.

Signs of easy expendability had been present earlier when he was only six months into his training. Sears had set up interviews with nine trainees shortly after the Yom Kippur War in October, 1973, and the resultant oil shortage and recession. Dennis went into the interview still full of confidence from college. That attitude apparently kept him in the running, but he felt bad about those who did not make it: three trainees who had bought cars and clothes and rented apartments with the assurance that they had a job.

Then Sears dismissed a friend's father who had worked seventeen years for them. "Their theory is the most controllable expense is payroll. So when times are tough, people go. And I was never able to forgive that. They have you over a barrel. And as you get older, the more dangerous it becomes because you've put in ten, twelve, fifteen years of your life, and they're going to wipe you out, financially, emotionally."

Dennis began rethinking his career goals. He wanted to be independent, his own boss. He returned to an earlier career ambition, law. In January, 1976, he sent out applications to three law schools: the University of Kansas; Washburn University, in Topeka; and the University of New Mexico. In April KU offered him money, and after mulling it over for a month, he accepted.

"There it was all over again. The only brown face in the classroom." The Bakke case about reverse discrimination was making news then. Classmates told Dennis the only reason he got in was because they had a quota to fill. He was not really

smart enough to be in law school; his LSAT (Law School Aptitude Test) scores were lower than those of everyone else.
Dennis laughed. "Welcome to KU law school."

Law school itself was enough for Dennis that first year without the taunts of his classmates. "The hardest thing I ever did
besides get a divorce. Incredibly hard." He pointed across the
room to a copy of *Webster's New Collegiate Dictionary,*
which he carried with him continuously the first three months.
"They were using words I hadn't used in over a year. I was
used to speaking Spanish 80 percent of the time."

"Didn't you have an Afro then?"

Dennis smiled and nodded. Studying day and night and
trying to be a good husband and a new father, he found his
personal habits began to slide. He never seemed to have time
to comb his hair. One day he got a perm. "I never had to
comb it. Just got up in the morning and shook it and was
ready to go."

Defiance, too, he figured, played a role in his new look.
"Just to be even more what they hated." He sighed. "Oh,
well."

As in sports, college, and business, Dennis's perseverance
and double effort would pay off in law school. His grades improved every semester, and he found a mentor in the Franklin
County county attorney he worked for during the summer between his second and third years. "He gave me the confidence,
he gave me room, he gave me—well, I guess that paternal or
maternal push that I seemed to require to do well. He opened
doors for me."

The third year Dennis shined. One day he was called on in
class and handled every question except one for forty minutes.
Another time he helped an unprepared classmate who had
made it clear the first semester that he was pro-Bakke. Dennis
was sitting next to this classmate when the teacher started to
drill him. "And he began to crumble. I was very prepared, and
so I whispered answers to him for fifteen or twenty minutes. I
took great satisfaction the entire time. And after class he told
me, 'Thank you.' And I said, 'You're welcome.' I didn't rub it
in. I just wanted him to think about it, how he thought we

couldn't do it, and here I bailed him out from embarrassment in front of all these people."

Dennis graduated from law school feeling pretty good, pretty cocky. But he was not one to rest on his laurels. In the spring of his last year of law school he had returned to repay his debt to the G.I. Forum, the organization that had given him his first boost in education. As guest speaker at the yearly banquet for Hispanic students, he gave this advice: "There are going to be times when you get scholarships or promotions or jobs. And some of your classmates or the people you work with are going to say, 'The only reason you got to med school or law school or any school or job is not because you're smart, but because you're a Mexican and there are quotas to make.' And if you believe that, they'll take away the sense of accomplishment that every human being wants. The only way to protect yourself is to always try your best. In the end, no matter who and how many tell you otherwise, you'll know in your heart that's not true." Dennis stopped to take a breath. "I had that speech in my heart for three years. I have copies." He laughed.

"Do you have a scrapbook?"

He nodded, a little sheepishly. One for his daughter and one for his son. "I really don't think their mother is going to leave them with an accurate impression of what I was about and what I was doing during this time. Because during law school and the year after is when my marriage came apart. I want them to be able to know and to see and understand what my feelings were, what my beliefs were, that I wasn't hotdogging it, running all over town—that kind of stuff. I want them to know I was an activist. I had some convictions, I had some beliefs, and I was out there fighting for them. So I do have scrapbooks—partly for vanity, but mainly for my children."

"Was your success in the Anglo world a factor in your divorce?"

Dennis drummed his fingers on the table for several minutes and then spoke slowly. "I think the failure of my marriage was the result of a difference in personal and, to a small extent, political values. My former spouse—and I'm trying to speak about this in a fair and detached way—had an interest in wealth. I did not. So it's kind of funny: she wanted me to be a lawyer, but not a legal-aid lawyer. She wanted me to be a private attorney and rake in the big bucks, which I had no desire to do. She could not understand why I would go talk to the school board about MACE (Mexican-American Committee on Education) when I could be wearing a three-piece suit and going out to the Country Club."

Dennis, though, felt the pull of family tradition. "I had always wanted to come back and fight like the old warriors," he said, referring to his father and the other Hispanic veterans who came back from World War II and demanded their rights. "If I can come back and fight the injustices that exist and give to this community in return for what they gave to me, then I'll be happy. Then I'll have a sense of accomplishment."

In August, 1979, ten years and two months after he first left for New Mexico, Dennis returned to Garden City to work for Kansas Rural Legal Services. During his absence from Garden City many things had changed, most of them for the better. His father had served on the city commission. "That was something he had in mind for a long, long time. I can remember being eleven or twelve, eating supper, and Dad talking about how he thought he could run for the city commission and win. I remember being surprised, probably not very optimistic, when I first heard he was running. I thought he could make it through the primary, and I thought he had a slim chance to make it on the third spot."

Hispanics had also made inroads into the marketplace. They were working in banks and radio stations and schools. As a child Dennis knew of only one business establishment owned and run by a Hispanic: a bar, noted for its shootings. He could now count fifty-eight businesses owned or run by Hispanics.

At the high school Hispanics were participating in all activities: debate, drama, music, and cheerleading. Eleven of them were on the football roster. At a disco dance he was impressed by the ease with which the students—blacks, whites, browns—danced with one another. In his day at sock hops Anglos were on the right, Mexicans on the left.

Much still remained to be done in the schools, though, Dennis felt. The dropout rate at the high school was forty to fifty percent for Hispanics, a failure he attributed to an inadequate bilingual program. One of his biggest cases to date was a bilingual education lawsuit against the school district. The sink-or-swim method simply will not work, he said. "Ideally, there is a time span in which you get the type of bilingual education that will allow you to learn English and allow you to develop other learning skills—say three, at the most four, years. Then you have to get out, get in the regular classroom. But the bilingualism will allow you to not lose out, lose interest, lose confidence, be stymied. That's what happened to my parents."

As when he was in McAllen, Texas, selling shoes, Dennis found his own knowledge of "the language" essential to his law practice. He estimated that it took him a year to a year-and-a-half to learn all the legal terms in Spanish. Once he did, though, cases that had perplexed others for months, even years, were cleared up easily. In one case a Spanish-speaking neighbor of his was notified that her Social Security benefits were being cut off for a year-and-a-half. On the basis of an interview held a few months before, with a translator present, they had determined that she owed them money. Looking at the forms that had been filled out and speaking with the woman, Dennis discovered that the answer to one question had been incorrectly translated. "That's not brilliant, but I was the only person able to get that information so that now she doesn't have to make that overpayment."

Many of Dennis's siblings also learned Spanish and used it in their professions. The oldest, a nun, was working as a certified midwife in poor neighborhoods and clinics, in Dallas. Three other sisters living in Garden City—a nurse for migrant health, a bilingual teacher, and an aid interpreter for the school district—used Spanish daily, as did another sister who worked for an insurance claims adjustor in Albuquerque. One of his brothers, a business reporter for the *Arizona Daily Star,* was one of a handful of reporters selected to spend a year studying in another country. He chose Mexico.

Knowing Spanish offered personal benefits as well for Dennis. "I think my ability to speak Spanish has brought me closer to the older members of my family—my aunts and uncles, my grandparents—who I can now speak to in their language much more than I ever could as a child."

"Then you don't feel success has alienated you from your family?"

He shook his head. "I have seen families, I guess, whose success in the non-Spanish-speaking arena has divided them from the home. But I think the challenge is on those people who have been successful in the non-Spanish-speaking world to bridge the gap that set them free in the first place." Most people who want to, he felt, find a way. "Especially here in Kansas. In the bigger places—like LA, New York, maybe some parts of Texas and New Mexico—that division might occur more frequently."

There was a sense of alienation, though, within the more established Hispanic community in Garden City. A new farm-machinery manufacturer and several beef-packing plants had brought new Chicanos into the area. "Before, we all knew each other and were very tight knit. We learned what to expect and what not to expect out of certain people and families. And now we have so many—from Texas, Colorado, New Mexico. We don't know any of their family histories, where they came from. Maybe there's some uneasiness amongst us now." The old East-side–West-side feud disintegrated as families moved out of their old neighborhoods and new Hispanics established themselves elsewhere. "In a way it's good. It pumps some new life into the community. There was literally a time when you knew every Mexican in town. Not anymore."

"Has your neighborhood changed?"

"Oh sure. It's changed."

"Gone downhill?"

Dennis laughed. "Yeah, what's become of the old neighborhood? It's just not the same anymore. Property values have gone down. . . . No, no. The complexion of our neighborhood has changed—literally. In late July I was walking to the park, and I saw all manner of people who all lived in this neighborhood—brown ones, white ones, black ones, Vietnamese. All right there in a two-block area."

"How does the Hispanic community feel about the Vietnamese in Garden City? Is there any resentment?"

"The resentment I get is why does the United States government do all that for those people—give them their papers immediately—when we have hundreds of children in the United States who are U.S. citizens but whose parents are not, or one parent is not, and they are forced to leave the country or have one or both parents leave the country. It doesn't make sense." But the resentment is not personal. "I don't hear jokes about pets, things like that." Dennis mentioned the efforts the Hispanic community had made to contact the Vietnamese and offer them help and to elicit their services for the school district.

Linguistically, the Vietnamese would adapt to the United States much quicker than the Hispanics, Dennis thought. Oceans separated them from their country and other native speakers, whereas Hispanics in Garden City could turn on their radios late at night and pick up a station from Mexico.

The existence of a new minority in town made Dennis feel like part of the old guard. He recalled one Sunday afternoon when he went downtown to see a matinée at the theater and found a Vietnamese film was being shown. "I guess I felt like a lot of English speakers felt when they went to the movies and it turned out to be Spanish night. But in a way I liked it; it was a little amusing. It made me feel good because it made me think that what I expect others to do for the Spanish speakers, I must now do for the Indo-Chinese."

At thirty-one Dennis Garcia had come a long way from the meek baseball enthusiast who was afraid to cross the tracks. Braces glittered on his front teeth, whose crookedness had made him self-conscious in high school. "I even heard it was chic," he said. Other discomforts of his youth had been taken care of as well. "I have a clean, no-holes pair of socks every day for two weeks. And gloves. You know when I was a kid,

I hated my hands. I didn't have any gloves. Now I have two or three pairs of gloves. And if the time comes when my son says to me, 'Dad, I need a pair of tennis shoes to go out for basketball,' I can do that for him. I am very comfortable compared to where I was at in my youth. Not rich. But man, I'm comfortable."

He paused a moment and shook his head. "Show me a Catholic, and I'll show you someone who knows how to feel guilty. But the thing is they never teach you what to do about your guilt." He chuckled and then grew serious as he mentioned being haunted by the troubles of his childhood friends. "When I was a kid there were a couple hundred kids who basically had the same environment, the same things I did. And in their lives there is a sense of emptiness, a sense of not being all that they could have been, of not getting a fair shot at it, of having difficult times at home, in employment, with the law, with the Church, with their family. And I have been spared. I have been lucky. I look at the guys my age and what they're doing and all the difficulties they're in, and I'm saying, 'Why was I lucky enough to miss all that? Why was I given the breaks to go to schools, to get the scholarships, to get the jobs? Why was I given the ability or the parents to tell me that it's not enough that you're good, you've got to be twice as good?' "

Devoting himself to providing equal opportunities for his people was Dennis's practical, rational way of dealing with his guilt. "The people I am principally concerned about are the poor, the Spanish speakers, the non-English speaking. If I can help, if I can give them the opportunity to develop, then I will feel I have met my life's purpose."

But there also seemed to be some version of Pascal's wager involved in his motivation. "You know at Saint Mary's we learned that everyone is given a mission. And if you don't do something with it, boy, you're going to pay hell—literally." He laughed.

"Don't get the wrong impression of what I'm telling you. Sometimes I don't do so well. I think of now . . . my marriage has come apart, my children are miles away from me. I've had my difficulties like everyone. I think I'm just trying to develop a level of consistency. Sometimes I don't practice what I preach. But just because I'm not successful all the time doesn't mean I give up on it."

CHAPTER 10

Making Waves on the High Plains

NO PASSENGER TRAIN STOPS in Pierceville, Kansas, anymore. Once a rival of Garden City for county seat and of Dodge City for the title of Cowboy Capital, Pierceville has never quite recovered or tried to recover since it was burned to the ground by Indians in 1874. At one time the train stopped there five times a day. Now only freight trains stop to load at the grain elevators. The passenger train thunders through at about eighty miles per hour twice a day, heading west toward Garden City in the early morning and east toward Dodge City late at night. Most passengers probably do not realize that out there in the dark lies a town and the studio for the only public radio station in southwest Kansas.

Turning south off Highway 50, between two grain elevators, one tired August day in 1982, I drove down the main and only paved street in Pierceville. To the right, large white capsules of anhydrous ammonia (liquid fertilizer) glowed in the sun. Down the road apiece, to the left, was a cemetery for abandoned and broken-down vehicles and plumbing. I counted three flatbed trucks, a van, at least a dozen cars, a lawnmower, a washer and dryer, a toilet, and a charred trailer. Six seemed to be the average number of vehicles, on or off blocks, for each household. Up ahead a red fire truck poked out of the weeds next to the community gym. Self-service, I had been

146

told: the keys were left in it for easy access; the last person to use it was responsible for filling it up with gas.

The unincorporated town was chosen as the studio site for KANZ, at least in part, because of its anonymity. The station founders knew they would have to attract a widespread audience in this sparsely populated area to be able to support the station and thus did not want it associated with a single, more populous small town. Still, looking at this town where each household had its own propane tank and junkyard made me wonder if the station manager—my brother, Quentin—did not feel some personal affinity for this place: it reminded me of my family's basement that was full of disassembled televisions, radios, and stereos while he was growing up.

Ahead of me a round-bellied man in his thirties, dressed in a T-shirt and jeans, stepped out of the Country Store, Pierceville's only retail business. I pulled over to the right and offered him a ride.

His shaggy mustache spread into a grin and covered the tops of his front teeth as he reached for the door. Sweat rolled down the sides of his face. "Say, do you think you could take me out to the transmitter site? I want to do a meter calibration and check the transmission-line pressure. But I need to stop at the station first. I'd really appreciate it."

Chuck Lakaytis, KANZ's engineer, shared a house with Quentin in the opposite direction, across the highway. The Even Couple, my mother called them—meaning Oscar rather than Felix. Chuck's car, a 1972 blue Pontiac, had sat in the weeds, Pierceville-style, for the last year or so.

I swung to the left in front of the former Pierceville grade school. A bent flagpole, two weary merry-go-rounds, and a fire-escape slide on the north side of the building remained as mementoes of the children who once trod these grounds. After the school district consolidated and children in Pierceville were bussed elsewhere, the building was abandoned for many years. In the late 1970s the station started renting it from the school district for a dollar a year. A large sign—"KANZ-FM: Pioneering Public Radio"—a glimpse of a satellite dish, and a communications tower poking up from the back were the only visible evidence of the changeover.

Chuck and I entered the studio, located in the newer, low-ceilinged part of the building. Striped carpeting led through a door and down a hallway, the left side of which was divided into cubicles for staff members. Large wooden mailboxes hung on the right wall for the staff; smaller honeycomb-shaped metal boxes hung on the left wall for volunteers. Down the hall the Teletype clacked, competing with the early Mozart on the air.

A sheet on the door to the left listed weekly cleaning duties for each staff member. Beyond stood an assortment of desks and file cabinets of varying styles and ages that served as the front office. A sunset painted in rectangular, polychromatic stripes decorated the north wall, and wheat poked out of a pipe section sitting atop a shelf. Because of the donations of material and labor by staff and volunteers, the conversion from grade school to radio station cost only about five thousand dollars instead of the projected fifty thousand dollars.

The room between the front office and control room served as a conference room. On the day I visited, it was doubling as a nursery for Fiona, infant daughter of Rachel Hunter—the announcer in the next room. Homegrown zucchini, brought in by a listener, sat on a large carpeted table in the center of the room. In the corner stood a three-and-a-half-foot antique radio donated by another listener. An aerial map of the nineteen-county listening area hung on the west wall.

I waved through the large window at Rachel, operations manager, who daily drove in from Dodge City, thirty-five miles to the east. She adjusted her headphones and the "On Air" sign flashed on above the door. I peered through the window at the winking green and red lights on the control board. Chuck's tour of the station always included a detailed description of what each light indicated, but it still looked like Christmas to me.

Chuck was gathering equipment in his office, an engineer's menagerie of wires and tubes and tools. A bookshelf near his desk included electronics reference books, as well as the Harvard Classics editions of Plato, Epictetus, and Marcus Aurelius; Modern Library editions of Aristotle and Aquinas; books by Keynes; the second volume of Newton's *Principia;* the CRC handbook of chemistry and physics (1968–69); and the *Oxford English Dictionary*. Before settling on engineering, Chuck had considered majors in physics, economics, and European intellectual history.

On the top shelf opposite the books, I spotted a large box of sanitary napkins.

"You mind explaining those?"

Chuck's eyes lighted up with glee, and he rubbed his mustache. "Those are used because they're lint free. When we clean the transmission lines you tie about ten of them on a rope and pull them through the transmission line. You know, I've often wondered what the woman in K-Mart thought when Molly and Steve Fenton and Steve Olson went into the checkout stand. They had, say, ten boxes of Maxi-pads, four pairs of rubber gloves, four scrub brushes, two big plastic washtubs, and a couple of gallons of muriatic acid. This woman just stared at them. I'm sure she thought they were setting up some kind of abortion clinic in town." Chuck sputtered with laughter.

The transmission line, bought secondhand, had not been the only cause of recurring technical snarls at KANZ. The antenna, bought brand new, had also caused its share of major difficulties. Between the two, the station had a rough start. Originally scheduled to go on the air for the first time in May, 1980, KANZ had to delay its debut until June 29. Even then it was broadcasting at only 60 percent of its full power (100,000 watts). Extensive testing in July revealed the problem to be somewhere in the 140-foot antenna and not in the transmission line as was previously thought. A three-month battle with the antenna company, in Indiana, ensued. When several holes the size of quarters were discovered in the outer conductor of the antenna, the company agreed to send replacement parts. They turned out to be a half inch too long. Not until October, six months after the anticipated sign-on date, was the station broadcasting at full power.

But their problems were not over. Shortly after six in the morning, January 20, 1981—the day Reagan was inaugurated and the hostages were freed—program director Molly Hoffman called Chuck to report that the transmitter would not go on. He arrived in a few minutes, checked the remote control and microwave equipment at the studio, and headed for the transmitter site at KGLD-TV, thirteen miles away. The VSWR light was on when he arrived, indicating that the transmitter had tried to come on but had shut down when the antenna began reflecting power back into it. After several attempts to get it to come on, he called Quentin. Together they managed to disconnect the transmission line and antenna and switch it to a "dummy load," a test antenna. It worked, indicating the problem was, as usual, either in the transmission line or the antenna. To further isolate the problem, they dispatched one person to a television station in Hays, two-and-a-half hours away, and another to Hutchinson, three hours away, to borrow test equipment. Later, in a program guide, Quentin wrote, "It all feels very much like being kicked in the stomach."

Other technical problems—winter ice storms that kept the station at low power until the ice melted off the antenna and a break in the power divider that caused the transmitter to shut off for several days—had kept Chuck sleepless, red eyed, and unshaven during much of his two years at the station. On this particular day, however, traveling the familiar road to the transmitter site, he was rested and clear eyed, and the steady hum of the FM band made the technical problems seem as invisible as the waves emitted from the tower ahead. A blue-grass ditty seeped out the car speakers and spilled over the fields of ripening corn and soybeans, challenging the buzz of an irrigation pump. Red-winged blackbirds flashed their identities as they alighted on telephone wires; hens ran nervously from the road as we passed by.

Climbing the orange-and-white, eight-hundred-foot communications tower that loomed ahead was a feat many of the staff members could claim. Chuck had scaled it several times, as had music director Steve Olson and volunteer Dennis Bosley. Molly Hoffman had made the trip part way up.

"I don't know what the deal with the antenna is," said Chuck—"if we just got a lemon or if we were squirreled around. But I do know that the station can't keep paying five thousand dollars every year to rebuild the antenna. Now if a crop duster would hit the tower and knock it off, we'd just call the insurance company."

"Has KANZ had an unusual number of technical problems?"

"Oh, Lord, no. At least not for a community public radio station. Most community stations are not put on the air with nearly as much organization and thought. At KOPN, in Missouri, where I was working before, things were always fritzing."

Before taking up with public radio, Chuck worked as a bio-medical engineer and drove a BMW. "When they lost their federal funding, I began to have deep questions about whether what I was doing made much sense—working on life-support systems for people in their eighties. I remember one particular project I worked on. We developed a circulatory-assist system, and the object was to keep the patient alive as long as possible so that it would look good for this doctor who was going to some conference. He was having a contest with other doctors. I just said to hell with it."

In the early 1970s Chuck turned instead to salvaging infant community public radio stations. When KOPN, in Columbia, Missouri, was struggling to get its start, he loaned them his stereo. He lost the stereo but gained a job.

In the first part of 1980 a KANZ staff member visited KOPN to check out their record collection and ran into Chuck. He told him about KANZ's technical problems.

"I told him, 'Well, if you can pay me my expenses, feed my face, and pay me a little money, I'll come out and put the station on the air for you.'"

A two-week stay in April turned into six weeks, and he was offered a job in August.

"I've been pleasantly surprised out here," Chuck said, as

we passed a field of wheat matted by the recent, unusual rains of the summer. People aren't nearly as narrow minded and dull as everybody else in the country thinks they are. I think it appears that way because of the geographical isolation."

Geographical isolation was what Quentin had had to contend with while growing up in and coming back to western Kansas. Before he left for college in the summer of 1972, there were only three public radio stations in Kansas—KANU, in Lawrence; KSAC, in Manhattan; and KMUW, in Wichita—all affiliated with universities, all in central or eastern Kansas, none of which he had heard.

"I guess I first became aware of public radio when I entered Antioch College, which had a station, WYSO, which at that time was a campus station. It was not affiliated with National Public Radio. But I was struck by listening to it, mainly because it sounded so completely different from any radio I'd heard before, not only in the types of music that were played but the fact that there weren't any commercials, that there were just lots of different people on the air. There was a lot of just playing on that station—some good and some bad—but all of it rather exciting and at a time, too, I suppose, when you're real open to that sort of thing."

Quentin leaned back in his chair, repeatedly smoothing the thinning, wispy hair on the back of his head with alternating hands. He had canceled three previous appointments with me before he was finally able to have this conversation.

During the winter quarter of his freshman year, while WYSO was preparing to become affiliated with NPR and was off the air much of the time, Quentin did some engineering work for them. The next year he worked for a public television station in Dallas. In fall, 1974, he transferred to Oberlin College, in Ohio, where he did some engineering for the college media center.

"When you look at it, I actually had very little contact with public radio. Up until KANZ was on the air I had never worked for a public radio station or even heard much public radio."

In the winter of 1976–77 he returned to Garden City to work on his senior project: a study of small-market (100,000 or under) radio stations—which at that time meant commercial.

"I wouldn't call it the prospectus for KANZ but sort of the thought-piece for it."

The first part of the project examined the cultural and historical roots of rural radio. "On the one hand, radio was seen as the great liberator of the farmer and the small town. They would really wax eloquent in the 1920s over it because now the poor, downtrodden farmwife could have the joys of music and literature and of knowing what was going on in the world, and it would relieve the drudgery and remove the isolation, and all those wonderful things—which were all true. Of course, it also had the effect of opening up the wide world, and that, combined with the development of the automobile and the changing economic ways of the country and everything else, just added to all the incentives to leave the rural area. A whole entertainment industry grew up around radio, and it was urban oriented essentially—very little local or rural input or control over it at all. The only real local input and control you got over radio was after television came along and radio was no longer a national medium. It had to go back to being a local medium. So actually radio improved for rural areas with the coming of television, although I think overall rural life declined."

The potential of rural radio had been largely neglected, however, as the second part of Quentin's study—a quantitative survey of two hundred small-market radio stations—showed. "There are a handful of good stations, but, by and large, commercial broadcasting in rural areas is a pretty marginal activity: very narrow range of programming, not a high level of diversity or competency, not even in all cases profitable."

The third part of his study comprised models for developing public radio stations in rural areas, to make them as common, say, as public libraries.

Quentin rose to fetch a beer from the refrigerator. "I'm real glad I did some of that theoretical thinking early on because it's real hard to think very theoretically about it when you're doing it."

On a July evening in 1975, while he was still in college, Quentin had gathered with several friends from high school and other natives of the area around my folks' dining-room table and formed a nonprofit corporation, Kanza (one of the spellings of the name of the Indian tribe for which Kansas is named). That was the first step to bringing public radio to southwest Kansas. Over the next couple of years some of the original founding members dropped out, taking full-time, full-paying jobs elsewhere. Upon graduating from Oberlin in 1977, Quentin had a job offer from the media center there, but he decided to come back and begin breaking out the pasture for grass-root support of public radio.

"Was it difficult to come back?"

"I probably felt a certain personal stigma about coming back. By all common perceptions, you know, a sign of making it would be not to be in the area, to be in a more urban setting, a more professional job setting. It was almost like, having gone away to school, having worked in an urban area like Dallas, I was stepping back—which happens fairly often, but I felt I was doing it at an early age. Also, just leaving most of the people I knew well. Even people I'd known well here weren't around because they'd gone off to bigger and better things."

"What about the people you knew at Oberlin? Were they surprised?"

"It was probably harder to explain to friends here. At Oberlin there was a lot of real support. They thought it was wonderful, mainly because they thought you were fortunate to have a place to go back to and a project like this to work on. Students, but even more so faculty, were very supportive of the idea."

Initial financial support for KANZ also came from outside sources. In February, 1978, Quentin sent off a three-inch-thick

application to the FCC for a license; in March of the same year
he delivered another three-inch-thick application to the HEW
office for a $106,000 matching construction grant. By late fall
Kanza had received both the license and the grant.

Folks at home were a little slower coming around. "I remember sometime early in 1979 I had just finished a spot on a
local commercial radio station explaining what public radio
was about and how much money was needed and a farm
type—seed cap, whole bit—came bounding in and slapped
the other person with me on the back and said, 'Well, hell,
I've already got a public radio and it didn't cost no hundred
thousand dollars either. I've got what's called a CB. You get
yourself one too.' That was the first clear public reaction we
got to the idea."

Other people confused public radio with public television,
which was also trying to get established at the same time in the
area (it later failed). Some did not know about the FM band.

A couple of disasters also provided setbacks, material and
psychological, before the station was on the air. In December,
1977, a fire in a minimall in downtown Garden City destroyed
one of the first Kanza offices. "Fortunately I hadn't unloaded
the five thousand brochures that had been sitting in the back
of my car for a couple of weeks, so I still had those," said
Quentin. The next year, in September, a Kanza Day celebration in Pierceville ended early. There were complaints about
the obscene lyrics sung by one band, and the toilets in the
school building were not working, forcing the Kanza people
to use those across the street in the community gym, where
the all-time Pierceville school reunion was underway. Such
goings-on did not sit well with either the Pierceville folk or the
administrators of the school district.

More direct opposition in the early days of KANZ came
from owners of a couple of area commercial radio stations. In
editorials they labeled KANZ "government radio" and ac-
cused it of not paying its own way because of its dependence
on federal funds. One even suggested people write their con-
gressmen and senators, asking them to rescind the grant.

"How do you justify spending government money?"
Quentin shrugged. "That's one of the things the government
is there for. One purpose of the government is redistribu-
tion of wealth—not so much equalizing incomes as to say
in a democratic society there are some things which are not
salable—roads, libraries, schools. They simply don't have
the profit incentive for which people will invest, yet they're
important."

"What about the editorial from the radio station that claims
they're already giving people what they want, that the purpose
of the media is to provide satisfaction for the majority of
listeners?"

"Well, from their point of view. Having listeners is only an
indirect goal of the commercial station. Their goal is to have
as many advertisers as possible. The way to have more advertisers is to have a larger audience; the way to have a larger
audience is to program something that appeals to the widest
number. I'd say something that 'satisfices' rather than satis-
fies—you know, you hear something you really like every
thirty minutes or so, which is enough to keep you listening."

"And from your point of view?"

"I'd say in a democratic society the major purpose of the
media should be to entertain and enlighten and inform—in
the broadest sense of the word. Which means, given the fact
there are a lot of frequencies—there are lots of means of deliv-
ering words and images—there's no need for anything to be
excluded."

A sample *Kanzan* guide indicated that little was excluded
from KANZ's format. The station offered a wide variety of
music—classical, opera, jazz, folk, bluegrass, ethnic, rock,
nostalgia, show tunes, and concert and big bands—as well as
radio drama, in-depth news, and public-affairs programming.
Seventy to eighty percent of the programming originated lo-
cally. A satellite dish, however, allowed the station to bring in
programming from any of twenty-four channels transmitted by
National Public Radio studios in Washington and thus pre-
vented the station from becoming what one staff member
termed a "glorified CB." The dish was placed in back of the

station, away from the road, to spare it the fate often met by
signs in the country—gunshot holes.

"How do you decide what to program? Do you try to reflect
or illuminate the tastes of the community?"

Quentin played with his beer tab, bending it either direction.
"I'd say it goes back and forth, and you're always somewhere
in the middle. Start with reflecting the community. Well, that's
a tough one because what's really the community? And is the
community a reflection of what's already available? Does the
community like country and western because it's what they've
grown up on or because they really like it? And who's to say
whether or not the community likes classical music when it's
never been heard? And what is reflection? Is it reflecting all
the little pieces out there or reflecting some average? So I don't
think there is such a thing as reflecting the community per se.
I think there is such a thing as trying to find out what the range
of interests is in the community which are not being addressed.
It's a real dynamic situation, going back and forth all the time.
And it'll drive you nuts. It really will."

Letters on file at the station indicated that KANZ listeners
were not shy about making their preferences known. Several
voiced standing complaints about programming. Too much
talk was a common one: ". . . by the time you have explained
the background on the music right down to the political attitudes of the composer, I not only have forgotten the title but
I'm getting ready to turn to another station." No jazz on the
Sabbath, please, wrote another: "Well, my idea of a relaxing
Sunday evening is shot when I snuggle into bed with a book,
turning on the radio, only to hear a tenor trumpeter blowing as
though he's 'peaking' on amphetamines." Several others ob-
jected to the five hours of Hispanic programming every Saturday afternoon. A few who were acquainted with public radio
stations elsewhere wanted an all-jazz or all-classical station.

The seeds of KANZ may have washed away or fallen on
stony ground in some places, but elsewhere they found fertile
soil and took root. Listeners from farms and close to forty

towns in Kansas; from three towns in Nebraska; from Walsh, Colorado; and from Perryton, Texas, wrote in praise of the station:

> Sunday A.M. Restful music, no Pepsi commercials. No electronic Soul Savers. It was very pleasant.
> Actually, I think this radio station is the best thing to come along since indoor plumbing.
> At the moment I am listening to the Chicago Lyric Opera in Liberal, Kansas, and enjoying it exceedingly although I am not that excited about opera. . . . We've felt undernourished with a steady diet of C and W, grocery store music, and "bottom 40."
> I started in the rabbit business about the same time you came on the air. . . . The rabbits and I especially enjoy any classical music. . . . I have deliberately scheduled a lot of rabbit breeding for Sunday morning. The music sets the mood.

Staff announcers offered me anecdotes illustrating the variety of listeners and tastes. Judy Seligson, who signed on the station at five-thirty every weekday morning, told of a phone call she received at six A.M.: "You know, I really like that tuba piece you're playing. I'm a farmer, south of Lakin, and my grandson always wanted to play the tuba but never did. And when you played that piece of music, it reminded me of that. What was that anyway?" Chuck received a less complimentary call one Saturday morning when he played some feminist folk songs: "This woman called up saying I'm spreading communistic, anti-Christian propaganda, striking at the very basis of the family structure and then finished off by saying, 'I don't think the women out here are ready for liberation yet.' I said, 'Well, give me the date, and I'll play the show again.'" Shawn Gilson, an eighteen-year-old summer intern, claimed he had a late Saturday night listener who called up regularly to ask, "Do you have any Jimi Hendrix for doing acid?"

For the twenty on-air volunteers like Shawn, the station offered a chance to share their own specialties. While still in high school, Shawn made a biweekly trip to Pierceville from Holdredge, Nebraska, some 200 miles away, to tape five-minute political commentaries as a sort of "Paul Harvey antithesis." Jim Adams, of Walsh, Colorado, 110 miles away, came in every month to tape a series of weekly shows called *Uncle Jack's Juke Joint,* based on his collection of rare rhythm-and-blues records. And on Sunday mornings Ursula Humburg, a German-born mother of two, left her farm, near Ness City, before dawn to host a classical music show with Quentin at seven. "Other people go to a psychiatrist. I come here to Pierceville."

"Well, I'd never put up Sheetrock before," said staff member Steve Olson, a tall, cheerful, young man originally from Iowa, when I asked him what he had learned since coming to KANZ. He was working at KAXE, in Grand Rapids, Minnesota—the first rural public radio station—when Quentin hired him as music director.

"On the phone Quentin said, 'We're not quite finished building it yet.' So I thought, you know, probably a little painting to do. Well, I walked into it—it looked like a bombed-out building. I was rather aghast. When I asked him where the record library was, he pointed to a closet where there were about fifty records."

The record library had since grown to cover one entire wall and part of another. Steve had grown too. He had worked from one May to the next, taking only one three-day weekend. "I learned how much I could work when I came here."

"Was it a difficult situation to walk into a place where people had never heard of public radio before?"

"It's been hard, and it's been simple. In a sense it's been an ideal situation—an audience that has no idea what you're trying to do, no preconceptions, no biases. You simply come in with this idealistic package, and you sell it: 'Here are all the great things about public radio; here's where you fit into it. What do you think? Should we do it?' And they said, 'Yeah, that sounds good. Let's do it.' That's very simplistic, but that's how it worked."

Judy Seligson first came to KANZ as an intern, from Oberlin College, in January, 1981. She recalled blanking out when she walked into the control room and saw all the buttons and gadgets. Her first time on the air she could not remember where she was from when Quentin asked her. "Mostly in four weeks I got a real sense of just how unique the project was for out here." After graduating in May, she returned the following August as a full-time staff member.

"I was looking for a small fishbowl, a small environment so that I could learn a lot of different things and actually make some decisions. I know I would rather be out in the middle of nowhere running a lot of the show than to be at some huge newspaper or radio station but limited in what I could do."

Rachel Hunter mentioned the democratic approach to salary and management. Linda Trower-Shuss, the development director, agreed. "I was at a radio conference recently, and someone asked me how I like working for Quentin, and I had never really seen myself as working *for* Quentin but rather *with* him."

Said Steve, "For me anyway, there's been more of a sense that my say has some sway. At a lot of community stations they try to do that, but it doesn't work always. I've heard people say in the last year it's getting less that way. You know, we'll come to a meeting and the new things will be laid down for us to absorb. A couple people have said to me, 'Whatever happened to "What about doing this?" ' But that's not very pronounced yet."

Program director Molly Hoffman, a soft-spoken young woman from Virginia, with definite tastes in classical and folk music, felt her decisions about what to program had often been overridden. "I will argue with Quentin, but he just keeps giving me the same reasons over and over. After the meeting I feel that I've said what I had to say, but it didn't make any difference."

"It's obvious he's had a lot of experience in debate," said Steve, grinning.

"What's it like to work with Quentin?"

"A lot of things. It's fun, it's intimidating, it's exhausting, it's creative. One of the things I've felt from time to time is that this radio station is his life and has been, obviously, for the last seven years or so. Since the station went on the air, we've all been working six days a week. But I would come out here at noon, and Quentin would have been here since eight or nine in the morning, and he'd still be here when I left at midnight. I just felt real intimidated.

"But there's also a sense of being in awe of someone who can do that. A lot of people helped him with this station, but without him it wouldn't be here because your average person isn't going to work eighteen to twenty hours a day for four or five years to see something happen. This community wouldn't have generated a public radio station within itself. It took someone like Quentin to go out and learn about public radio, but who had grown up here and knew the area and knew the station would work here and knew how to make it work here. He had a lot of things going for him—even though he had frizzy hair and wire-rimmed glasses."

Steve paused, smiled broadly, and creaked back in the old desk chair Quentin had appropriated from home.

"He's an interesting combination of extreme intelligence and drive and energy and, as we like to say, total air headedness. On the conceptual side he's very powerful and very creative; but he's forever searching for his car keys, he forgets cups of coffee all over, he forgets appointments. On the day-to-day detail level he's hopeless. His car looks like a warehouse. Someone once said about Quentin and Molly that you don't know where they're going, but you know where they've been because of all the stuff in their cars."

For Molly, who, along with Steve, was the longest term staff member besides Quentin, the differences between Quentin and her had come to outweigh their similarities. Less impressed with the station, she was more concerned about its effect on the people involved. Overwork and underappreciation had taken their toll. "I think zeal for a project often precludes sensitivity to the individuals involved. And I know I'm not the only one who feels that way. There are volunteers who do, too."

"The station is the cause," said Steve. "It's always a matter of us giving to the station a lot of ourselves and our work and not so much what we're going to get out of the station. People don't get complimented on their jobs; you take everybody for granted. You really have to devise your own self-satisfaction regimen so you know for yourself."

"How would you describe staff morale right now?" I asked Quentin late one night in Pierceville.

"Pretty burned out. Just plain weariness—working hard for a long while and knowing it's not going to let up. Everyone's pretty considerate on how they let it out. Nobody's mean. I think there's a feeling among some that they've reached their limitations here, it's time to move on."

"What about yourself?"

"I sometimes think—and maybe they're more vain feelings than anything—that my real talents and abilities lie perhaps in a little more specialized area, and being spread so thin, you can't really have a chance to excel at anything. There will be days when I can generate a lot of great ideas about things we ought to do, but when you have to implement them all yourself, when everybody else has their own responsibilities, when you don't have some support staff to make things happen quickly, to follow through on your ideas, it's frustrating. And just having the space to think. Like when I was out of town these past four days, I wrote out an outline for a couple of foundation-grant proposals. Well, I don't know when I'll be able to work from those notes into the proposal. It's probably an afternoon's work. The problem is finding an afternoon and finding it unencumbered. That sort of writing has to be inspired. And when you're hassled by details, it's hard to be inspired."

A train rumbled by. Then the still of the August heat returned.

"What do you miss, working so hard and living so far from a city?"

"The anonymity. Don't always miss it, but sometimes miss it. The variety of people, even if you don't directly deal with them—just having them there to look at. The variety of things to do—simple, straightforward things like films and books. I don't read as much as I'd like to. I miss not working for somebody, someone who clearly has a lot of expertise that you really want to learn from. You know, apprenticing under them. Also, there's some relief in that structure because you know what's expected of you and it's easier to measure your progress and easier to get your gratification. I feel like I've almost skipped a step."

"Has it been worth it? Would you do it over again?"

Quentin shook his head wearily. "I don't know. I've thought about it and never come up with a satisfactory answer."

Twice a year, for a period of ten consecutive days, staff members and volunteers at KANZ put aside their own reservations about the station and concentrated on only one aspect of public radio: fund raising. Memberships rather than commercials are public radio's means of covering operating expenses. For twenty-five dollars a year a listener became a member of KANZ and received the monthly program guide. Premiums, such as T-shirts and bumper stickers, accompanied pledges for higher amounts.

Marathon fever reached its peak during the October, 1982, pledge drive, however, when people were calling in with answers rather than pledges. Lights flashed, phones rang, people ran back and forth between the control room and performing studio during the hour-long trivia contests featured every night.

An area college biology teacher and a machinist from Garden City, who was dressed in a red, white, and blue kilt, served as quizmasters on the night that I visited. "What is the real name of the *Merrimack?*" "How high can a crab louse jump?" "What insect was used in surgery in World War II?" "What is spyhopping, and what is the name of a Kansas animal that does it?" Teams from surrounding towns and farms— the Boothill Gravediggers, the Liberal Conservatives, the Terrible Swedes, a contingent from Richfield (who went through seven exchanges to reach Pierceville) called in their answers and racked up their points. A boy about ten, playing without a team, called up and guessed at all the number questions: "Is it forty-six?" "1924?" "Thirty-three? . . . Aw, shucks."

At the mike, rubbing his hands up and down his jean-covered thighs, Quentin was in top form as referee. "Hello, you're on the air. You're on the air." "That's two for the Terrible Swedes, four for the Boothill Gravediggers." "Hello, you're on the air."

During a past marathon, when teams were determined by age, Quentin greeted a woman caller, "Oh, I know you. You're that woman from Morton County."

"No, I'm your mother from Finney County."

"Should I put you in the under-thirty or over-thirty group?"

With each marathon local support for the station had increased. The current membership was five times the national average, and the average contribution was 60 percent higher. The listening area, however, was considerably smaller than average, only 130,000. One study indicated that a minimum market of 400,000 was needed to make such an operation feasible.

The goal for the marathon in October, 1982, was the highest ever: $54,000. Previous marathon goals had been more modest—$15,000 the previous spring—based more on what the station thought it could raise than on what was actually needed.

The sharp increase in the current marathon goal reflected not only confidence in the strength of local support but also cutbacks in other funding sources. Federal support for operating expenses had dropped by half every year since the station had been on the air. From the summer of 1980 through the summer of 1981, the Corporation for Public Broadcasting and three CETA positions supplied 48 percent of the total operating expenses. A cut by one-third in the CPB money was expected the next year, but the termination of the CETA positions in March—shortly after Reagan's inauguration—was not expected and brought federal support down to 22 percent. In this third year of operation federal support would drop to 11 percent.

Expenses in the meantime continued to rise. The price of a favorite program, *A Prairie Home Companion*, carried by satellite, was raised from $10 to $20 weekly. In addition, American Public Radio, the program's distributor, was charging $850 a year for a required membership. The total yearly cost for keeping this one program on the air represented a 363 percent increase or two-thirds of KANZ's total program acquisition budget. In the past public radio had been considerate of the wide variation in budget and market sizes among stations and had made appropriate accommodations. This new attitude, explained Quentin in a program guide, seemed more akin to that of commercial radio: to charge all the market would bear.

With federal support drying up and no institution to fall back on, Quentin was hoping to find support from the state. Though Kansas had no provision for funding public radio, it did provide forty thousand dollars the first year as starting funds. It gave another ten thousand dollars for a plan to widen the listening area and thus the potential sources of revenue by installing repeater translators in Hays, Colby, Liberal, Ashland, Ness City, Elkhart, Goodland, Oakley, and Dodge City, Kansas; Lamar, Colorado; and Guymon, Oklahoma.

Local underwriting was another source the station was pursuing. Originally intended to provide 40 percent of the budget, it had fallen short of expectations, probably providing closer to 25 percent. "Being in a rural area, the station does not have access to large company matching grants," said Carlene Schweer, the station's underwriting director. "Also, times are hard, and people are cutting back—even our current underwriters."

A large, friendly woman, Carlene grew up on an area farm, the oldest of three girls. "I was my daddy's boy, and by all rights I probably should have been a boy." The most recent member of the staff, she had sold memberships to the Chamber of Commerce for twelve years and before that had worked for Merle Norman Cosmetics. "When I first walked in here, I wasn't sure I wanted to work where people dressed so casually. Now, look at me. I've had to buy a whole new wardrobe—of jeans."

During the marathon I noticed that she stayed clear of the mike. "Don't you like being on the air?"

"No. Not just no, but hell, no. It is not my favorite thing at all. Let me work behind the scenes and work one to one with people."

Other staff members, along with volunteers, took turns pitching on the air from 5:30 A.M. to 12:00 A.M. Quentin used his stint as an opportunity to reminisce about the early days of the station, when it was little more than a phone listing: "I remember when I knew all the members by memory. Then I needed a couple sheets of paper—which I usually lost. Now I don't know nearly all of them."

Later, during a lull in his shift at the mike, Chuck tired of the Jeffersonian appeal. "The next person who calls in with a fifty-dollar pledge will receive not only a T-shirt but I will also tell them the story of my Lithuanian ancestors who ran elephants for Hannibal. Complete with Latin quotations."

Quentin, pacing behind the window in the conference room and eating a stale doughnut, frowned. A phone rang.

By Sunday, October 24, the last day of the marathon, *A Prairie Home Companion* had been saved. Molly Hoffman had left for Virginia to be married and from there would travel to Europe with her husband and her hard-earned savings. And the ten-year-old boy had scored a few points in the trivia contest, thanks to anonymous callers who started calling in answers in his name.

The station, however, was still a few thousand dollars short of its goal. People called in increasing their twelve-by-twelve memberships ($12 a month for a year) to fifteen-by-twelves. Dennis Bosley—farmer, former president of the Kanza board of directors, and veteran tower climber—promised to kick in the last $100. A matching grant doubled every pledge for a few hours. Then at ten minutes until three a cheer erupted over the air: KANZ had met its $54,000 goal. Calls continued to trickle in, and the final figure was $54,838 from over eight hundred individuals, almost half of them new contributors.

During his shift the next morning Quentin played his Bob Dylan records from high school and then took off for Colby, Kansas, in his orange Fiesta to promote the translator project. "There are a lot of places where the station is real vulnerable." He mentioned staff salaries, equipment depreciation, and disasters.

The car bumped over the railroad tracks and halted at the intersection of the highway and the Pierceville Road. Since the station had been on the air, Broadcast Plaza, as KANZ's return-address label dubbed this road, had become a familiar thoroughfare for staff members and volunteers who drove in from towns and farms, near and not so near. A traffic counter reported an increase of ten to fifteen cars a day at the intersection since the station had been on the air.

Quentin turned onto the highway, the distance increasing between him and the station. Seven years before, he had started out something like the boy guessing random numbers during the trivia contest. The station had been an idea, a grant proposal, brochures. Once he was behind the mike he still could not see who his broadcast was reaching. But just as strangers had started phoning in answers for the boy, so strangers from towns Quentin had never heard of a few years before had started donating their money and time, producing their own shows, and designing their own plans for KANZ.

"It's not his station anymore," said Judy Seligson. "But it will always be his dream."

CHAPTER II

Afterword

I WROTE THESE CHAPTERS in 1982 and 1983. Since that time a few tentative signs that the water situation is improving have appeared: the Arkansas River has returned, the depletion of the Ogallala Aquifer has lessened, and fewer acres of corn have been planted. In the spring of 1985 melting mountain snows and heavy rains, rather than political ploys, persuaded officials at the John Martin Reservoir, in Colorado, to open the gates and release the excess water. Area newspapers tracked the daily progress of the Arkansas River across southwest Kansas. KANZ sponsored a contest, offering thirty dollars to the person who came closest to guessing the date water would reach the Pierceville bridge ("Never" was the most common answer). National Public Radio aired a feature, and the *Washington Post* sent out a reporter (who wrote that there had been no water in the river since the flood twenty years before). On a visit home that year, I saw people out with their sailboards and canoes and rafts and fishing rods, celebrating the river's homecoming. Water on the ground—it was enough to make any western Kansan's heart soar, even if we suspected it would soon be sucked up by the irrigators and the sun.

Perhaps some of that water replenished the Ogallala Aquifer. Figures for the two years immediately preceding the river's return indicate that the aquifer declined annually by only a half inch or less—one-third of the average annual rate of decline since 1966. Statistics for individual wells, however, paint a less cheerful picture. During 1984 nearly all the wells in the southwestern part of Finney County declined at a much greater rate than the annual average—a few by as much as seven or eight inches. And for some wells in neighboring Haskell, Grant, and Stanton counties, nothing short of a monsoon could begin to replace the hundred-plus feet of water that have been mined in less than twenty years.

The amount of irrigation, particularly in Finney County, has decreased significantly. In 1982 nearly 90 percent of the potentially irrigable acres in Finney County were in production; in 1983 and 1984 that percentage dropped to just over half (approximately 100,000 acres less than in 1982). Corn has shown the biggest decrease, from 96,000 acres in 1982 to 52,000 acres in 1983 and 50,000 in 1984. In the late 1970s corn constituted over half the irrigated acres in Finney County; in 1983 and 1984 it accounted for just over a third. The percentage of irrigated wheat, on the other hand, has increased—from a low of 20 percent to over 50 percent.

Figures, of course, say nothing about why farmers are growing less corn. The reasons probably have less to do with posterity and ecology than with short-term economics. (Irrigators showed so little support for a proposed groundwater-use control area along the Arkansas River that the local groundwater management district withdrew its request.) The year corn production fell so sharply, 1983, was also the year of the Payment-in-Kind (PIK) program, whereby the federal government paid farmers—in grain—to take a percentage of their land out of production. Corn prices were also low during these years.

At the state level, the Kansas Water Office is working on a comprehensive Kansas Water Plan. Its July, 1986, working draft of a report on the Upper Arkansas Basin focuses on groundwater deficits and recommends a return to dryland farming and crops more suitable to a dry climate. A Kansas House resolution seeks financial incentives from the federal government to make such a conversion. The plan shares some of the goals of the PIK program: to improve market prices by reducing the amount of surplus grain. A reasonable solution, it would seem. But, at least in the case of the PIK program, it has proved to be expensive and fruitless—or rather too fruitful: Kansas produced its second largest ever wheat crop during that year. In a world where bumper crops feed neither the farmer nor the starving, who can predict what will work and what will not?

Against this backdrop of economic turmoil and ecological uncertainty, the lives of the people I interviewed have continued to change. Jay Brown is no longer either a farmer or a bachelor. In May, 1986, he married high school classmate Becky Frazier. She spent the summer in Aspen, Colorado, as a violinist at the Aspen Music Festival, while Jay worked his last harvest. He wrote to me at the end of July, shortly before he headed for UCLA law school:

> It's true. I am off to Los Angeles the day after tomorrow, so I am packing and preparing like crazy. All the books had to be boxed up and taken up to Mom and Dad's attic. That was a back-breaker and we still have to move some of the furniture.
>
> It is pretty sad to move. Our family has lived in this house for nearly fifty years and the idea of it standing empty is very painful to me. But, there it is. I'm voting with my feet as Ronald Reagan would put it. Off to the land of sun and roller skates to learn the lawyering trade. It has been hectic around here waiting to hear if UCLA was going to give me enough financial aid so that we could afford to go out there. They have, and just in the nick of time. I begin a special two-week summer session on Aug. 2 designed, I think, to give a head start to ex-farmers and others the Law School believes may turn out to be clinkers.
>
> Farming is just out. I've given it a good shot for five years now (much longer of course, but five years since McGill). There is just no way to carry on, federal programs or not. Besides, Becky is definitely not farm-wife material. I decided to go to law school because I had never done anything but farm and go to school and I do not, therefore, possess a great number of marketable qualities. I thought about doing grad work in history and got into the U. of Chicago, but these people can't make a living so law it is.
>
> I don't know if we will ever be back in Kansas, somehow I doubt it. Visits, of course, but I do not see us moving back home.

The career Becky wants to follow and the career I have chosen make it unlikely.

So, I don't know. I hope I can figure out this law business. Oh, by the way, you might mention that I now have around thirty cats and only three of them are yellow. I have every other possible color combination, but just a few yellow ones. I hope Dad will come down and feed them after I leave, but I am less than sanguine about this.

Jay Brown is not the only person to leave the area and take up law. Rodney Hoffman wrote to me in the midst of studying for the Missouri bar exam. In 1983, after he lost the 1982 state representative election, Rodney, Barb and their two boys moved to Lawrence, where Rodney started law school at the University of Kansas. Barb taught learning-disabled students at two small rural high schools, a few miles north of Lawrence. Upon graduating in May, 1986, Rodney joined a medium-sized (eighteen-member) law firm in Kansas City. Barb planned to work only as a substitute teacher for the 1986–87 school year so that she could stay home with their new daughter, Emily, whom they adopted in February, 1986, at age ten months. After the school year they hoped to move closer to downtown Kansas City.

Dennis Garcia, already a lawyer when I interviewed him in 1982, has changed both his marital status and location. In the fall of 1983 he married Pamela Lekey, from Cimarron, Kansas, whom he met at his daughter's parent-teacher conference. The previous winter Dennis had developed a form of arthritis that caused him severe pain in his right hip. It is aggravated by cold, wet weather and rapid changes in weather ("I swear I could feel a snowfall coming two days before its arrival because my bones ached," he wrote to me). So he and Pamela moved to Tucson, Arizona, where the hot, dry weather and his daily medication keep him comfortable. He has not lost his enthusiasm for baseball: "I must have played over 1,200 organized games, and I still look forward to playing."

In Tucson, Dennis works for Legal Aid—a cause he still believes in deeply: "Fortunately, Congress has seen fit to keep life in the words 'and justice for all,' as opposed to the Administration's proposed 'and justice for all who can afford it.'" The low salary and the growing size of his family, however, have caused him to keep his eyes open for opportunities to combine his business and law backgrounds. When he wrote to me in 1986, he and Pamela had one son and were expecting another child. His daughter from his first marriage was also living with them. In October, 1985, Dennis's father, D. C. Garcia—the source of much of his determination and inspiration—died. "I have thought of him daily since," Dennis wrote. "For many months after, things were a little out of sync."

Public radio station KANZ has also undergone many changes since my visits there in 1982. Staff members no longer take turns cleaning the studios since outside help has been hired. An organized group of volunteers has eliminated the need for last-minute family sessions of assembling, folding, stapling, and labeling program guides. Marathons are now called "membership drives."

One key to increasing the station's membership has been the installation of twelve translators on top of grain elevators and specially constructed towers. This network of low-power transmitters rebroadcasts KANZ's signal at different frequencies, dramatically improving reception in several communities. Twice a day KANZ announcers must give the station ID for all twelve sites: Liberal, Elkhart, Ashland, Dodge City, Ness City, Tribune, Goodland, Colby, Oakley, and Hays, Kansas; Guymon, Oklahoma; and Lamar, Colorado. The station has permits and federal funding for an additional five translators. The translators, Quentin told me, "made all the difference in the world. We might not have been able to make it without them."

Membership peaked early in 1985 at 2,600, Quentin estimated. In the summer of 1986 it stood around 2,200. He attributed the decline to the farm economy and the "aging factor." "Being on the air for six years, the station is no longer new or unique—there is no urgency to join. It's going to be around. There were extraordinary contributions from people of limited means in the first few years."

Quentin hoped the slump would be offset by the construction of KZNA, a 100,000-watt, fully licensed repeater station, in Hill City, Kansas. KZNA has no studios, but the transmitter, along with additional translators, will extend KANZ's coverage across northwest Kansas. Together, KANZ and KZNA (known as "High Plains Public Radio") should boost the potential listening audience from 165,000 to 240,000.

On-air volunteers continue to share their voices and diverse interests with the station. Jim Adams still hosts the weekly rhythm-and-blues and rock show, *Uncle Jack's Juke Joint,* which is the longest running show produced by a volunteer. And he still drives over a hundred miles, one way, to the studios, though he has moved from Walsh, Colorado, to Hoxie, Kansas. Other volunteers have moved out of KANZ's listening range. Many listeners miss the pleasant German accent of Ursula Humburg, who drove ninety miles to Pierceville every Sunday before dawn to co-host a classical music program. In 1986 she and her family quit farming and moved to Lawrence.

Staff members have also scattered. Molly Hoffman Crook moved to Cedar Falls, Iowa, where she is senior producer for folk music at KUNI, and Rachel Hunter is in Lawrence, where she is fine arts director at KANU. Around Christmas, 1984, after a series of farewell parties extending over several months, Chuck Lakaytis departed for Ketchikan, Alaska, to become chief engineer at public radio station KRBD. Steve Olson left KANZ to become a jazz announcer at WUFT, in Gainesville, Florida, returned to KANZ as music director, and is now director of programming for Vermont Public Radio.

Of the 1982 staff, only one remains at KANZ: Judy Seligson. Since her days as a student intern, Judy has held the most positions at KANZ: morning announcer, news director, program director, and station manager. In May, 1986, she completed a year-long training program in station management— one of seven grants awarded nationally by the Corporation for

Public Broadcasting. After a tour of China, Japan, and Hong Kong in the summer of 1986, she took over Quentin's job as executive director.

Quentin left in August, 1986, to participate in a two-year Masters of Public and Private Management program at Yale. When I talked with him early in August, he was sorting through nine years of station files. Judy's training and wide experience with the station and area, the addition of KZNA, and $35,000 in operating funds from the Kansas legislature, he felt, would keep High Plains Public Radio on steady ground. He was less certain of his own future. He hoped to remain in rural development, working with community or economic entities, both public and private. Though he was looking forward to returning to a rich academic environment, leaving was not easy: "I already sort of miss the area and I haven't even left it."

Skip Mancini continues to thrive in southwest Kansas. She resigned from the city arts program and took a full-time position as director of drama and dance at Garden City Community College. When I heard from her in 1986 she was working on a fall production of *Quilters*. ("Not to worry," she wrote me, "because the patchwork quilts will be awe-inspiring, not cute!") The choice initially created some stir because the play features an all-female cast, but she predicted it would be tremendously popular. She had cast females from ages six to seventy, many of them farm women with no previous acting experience. Her plans included "wrapping" the entire set loosely in a burlap-type material—like a George Segal sculpture—to give it a fibrous look. And she was figuring out the choreography to bring one of her images to life: having the characters make a huge cat's cradle with their feet.

Her long-term plans included more community involvement with the arts and offering children's classes—which she had to give up the previous year. She was also compiling her class plans and exercises into a manuscript, hoping to publish it and travel around the country as a guest artist. Her husband, Vincent, was busy with several projects in different areas of the state. "All this leaves precious little time at Prairie Swift, where finishing up projects and landscaping goes on forever, all the while fighting the grasshoppers, wind and weather," she wrote to me. She added, "We both have no regrets about coming back, and staying. With the introduction of VCR equipment, we now even have a small library of foreign films—the thing we missed most when we first came here. My only regret is that I cannot live life without sleep, since there is so much to do yet and I have this nagging feeling that I will run out of time."